EUROPE UNITED?

Europe United?

The European Union and the Retreat from Federalism

Michael Welsh
*Chief Executive, Action Centre for Europe, and
Research Associate, University of Central Lancashire*

Foreword by

The Rt Hon Sir Leon Brittan, QC
Vice-President, European Commission

St. Martin's Press
New York

St. Martin's Press, Scholarly and Reference Division,
175 Fifth Avenue, New York, N.Y. 10010

First published in the United States of America in 1996

Printed in Great Britain

ISBN 0–312–15937–4 (cloth)
ISBN 0–312–15938–2 (paperback)

Library of Congress Cataloging-in-Publication Data
Welsh, Michael, 1942–
Europe united? : the European Union and the retreat from
federalism / Michael Welsh ; foreword by Leon Brittan.
p.   cm.
Includes bibliographical references and index.
ISBN 0–312–15937–4 (cloth). — ISBN 0–312–15938–2 (paper)
1. European federation.   2. European communities.   3. European
Union.   I. Title.
JN15.W455   1996
341.24'2—dc20   95–51174
                                                      CIP

JN
15
.W455
1996
7eb.1999

For G

Contents

Foreword

Europe today stands at an important crossroads. Behind us we have the Maastricht Treaty with all the innovations which it introduces, from EMU and increased powers for the EP, through to the creation of the intergovernmental 'pillars' for foreign and security policy and home affairs and justice policy. Ahead of us we face the challenges of the 1996 IGC, the need for Europe to develop a coherent defence policy for the post cold war era, and most significant of all, the need for Europe to enlarge eastwards.

Anyone like Michael Welsh, who is an insider in Europe, well understands the important role which the institutions of the EU play in how Europe and its policies develop – from the question of who proposes decisions through to who has the final say. But too often it is impossible for those who are not directly involved to appreciate exactly how decisions are taken or to understand how the characteristics of intergovernmentalism, in the form of personalities and domestic politics, have blended with the legal order of the Treaties and the European Court of Justice in order to produce the EU we know today.

Europe United? is therefore an extremely important text both for those who are students and practitioners of EU politics and those who are just interested bystanders. Moreover, because Michael Welsh leavens the sometimes indigestible subject-matter of EU institutional affairs with personal observation and anecdote, it is also one of the clearest and most readable texts around on Europe's institutions. I thoroughly recommend it.

LEON BRITTAN

Preface

This book is based on a course of lectures delivered to third-year students of European Studies at the University of Central Lancashire in the Autumn of 1994. In the course of preparing these I was struck by the dearth of popular material on the European Union; there is very little between the doctoral theses that are present in abundance on university bookshelves on the one hand, and tabloid trivia on the other.

European politics are widely regarded as grey and boring. My personal experience suggests the contrary, the political history of Britain since 1973 is inextricably bound up with the European Union, which has been a source of controversy and division in Britain since the year we joined. Europe along with the Health Service and Education has become one of the great totems in British political life and we need to understand the issues much more clearly if we are not to be swept away on the flood-tide of emotion and patriotism that it so easily evokes.

I have written this book with two audiences in mind. First it is for students who need a primer on the European institutions, written in accessible language and containing the basic references they need to complete their syllabus. It is also intended for the general reader who wants to understand the issues better so that he or she can make up their own minds free of the froth and emotion that so sadly warp reporting of these vital questions. In doing so I have tried to convey something of the colour and excitement that, contrary to the received wisdom, characterizes European politics. The British are brought up to believe that political drama begins and ends with the House of Commons; it is true that Question Time is a special form of political theatre but this should not blind us to the big personalities, Kohl, Thatcher, Delors and Mitterrand who walk the European stage, or to the issues which have a direct bearing on all our futures.

The European Union is the biggest political issue of our time and we need to understand it and appreciate the colour and excitement that underlie the grey exterior.

Europe United? starts with an account of the origins of the European Community and its institutional structure. The next four chapters look at the institutions and their functions against the background of developments in the eighties. Chapter 6 covers the period from 1989 to the conclusion of the Maastricht Summit in 1991, the next four deal in turn with the European Community itself, Common Foreign and Security Policy, Defence and Monetary Union. Chapter 11 takes us from the 1992 to the inauguration of the Santer Commission in January 1995.

I am particularly grateful to Sir Leon Brittan for writing the Foreword and to Professor Stanley Henig and members of the Department of European Studies at the University of Central Lancashire for their encouragement and support. Dr Timothy Bainbridge and Mr Graham Bishop have read parts of the typescript and made a number of helpful suggestions; it goes without saying that the opinions expressed are entirely my own as are any errors or omissions that may disfigure the text. Above all thanks are due to my wife, Jenny Welsh, who has painstakingly vetted the typescript and been my unfailing support and inspiration in good times and bad.

Whittle-le-Woods
4 June 1995

1 'Ever Closer Union': Origins and structure of the European Union

The quotation which forms the title of this chapter is taken from the first preamble to the Treaty of Rome which was signed on 25 March 1957 and established the European Economic Community. Taken together, the eight points of the preamble form an elegant and succinct statement of the Community's general objectives setting out the ambitions of the Founding Fathers for anyone who can be bothered to read what is there. The ideal of an 'Ever Closer Union', a process of evolution by which formerly hostile nation states are drawn together until finally they become integrated in a single political, economic and social entity, was the inspiration then and remains the motive force behind the European Union today. Indeed the first preamble to the Treaty of European Union concluded in Maastricht in December 1991 speaks of marking, 'A new stage in the process of European integration.'

A realization that integration is the central and explicit object-ive of the Treaties is essential to understanding the workings of the EU.[1]

The Founding Fathers who put their names to the Treaty of Rome had all been concerned with the reconstruction of their countries following the catastrophic Second World War. Every country of the original six had experienced the horrors of milit-ary defeat and occupation, the loss of hundreds of thousands of lives and the physical destruction of entire towns and cities. The deployment of V2 rockets by Germany, followed by the first, and so far only, use of atomic weapons at Hiroshima and Nagasaki made people realize that the next war was likely to be the last one, the destruction of civilization itself was a real possibility. The people of Europe had peered into the abyss and this was the time for a new political order which would banish the horrors for ever.

Since war was the product of rivalry between nation states, the only way of eliminating it was to bring those rivalries under

1

some kind of supranational control. This objective was explicitly set out in the preamble to the Treaty establishing the European Coal and Steel Community (ECSC) signed in 1951:

> Resolved to substitute for age-old rivalries the merging of their essential interests, by now establishing an economic community, the basis for a broader deeper community among peoples long divided by bloody conflicts, *and to lay the foundations for institutions which will give direction to a destiny henceforward shared.* (My italics)

The last phrase is the key. The history of the nineteenth century is littered with failed attempts at establishing some kind of European political order, starting with the Concert of Europe, 1815, right through to the foundation of the League of Nations in 1919. In each case the partnership had depended on governments recognizing that they had a common interest in establishing a framework for the orderly conduct of international relations and the settlement of disputes; each one collapsed when one or more of the states concluded that their national interest was better served by aggression than diplomacy. Nationalism required each state to put its own interests first; if these could not be secured by agreement with other countries pursuing their own interests with equal conviction, war was the only option. As Clausewitz pointed out, 'War is diplomacy carried on by other means.'

By contrast with the failings of intergovernmental co-operation, the experience of the allied governments during the war had showed that they could work together effectively, provided that the shared objectives were clear and compelling and the infrastructure for joint decision-making was in place. In spite of the obvious tensions, the Unified Command had been the instrument of liberation and there had been a remarkable degree of co-operation between the Allies in the post-war period. This owed much to the dominance of the United States and the lengthening shadow of the Soviet Empire, but it is easy to see why supranationalism was so appealing. In drafting the ECSC Treaty, Jean Monnet and his collaborators were trying to find common objectives that would transcend the national interest and create a supranational tier of government dedicated to their achievement. In so doing they were replicating their experience in domestic politics. During the post-war period the Continental democracies found themselves facing not just the external threat of Soviet expansion, but an internal threat as well in the shape of powerful Communist Parties dedicated to replacing the established order with a one party socialist state. Konrad Adenauer in Germany, Alcide de Gasperi in Italy, Robert Schuman in France and Paul-Henri Spaak in Belgium had all played key roles in building broad-based coalitions, cutting across traditional party differences, with the intention of permanently excluding the Communist Party from government. They had built their political careers on co-operation and compromise and the ECSC Treaty was an attempt to apply the same principles on an international scale.

The ECSC was intended to be the first step in a rapid process of political integration. Coal and steel industries were selected as the test-bed because they were considered essential to industrial and economic recovery and because rearmament could not be achieved unilaterally if they were under common control. The lessons of the thirties were fresh in everyone's mind.

The next step was to have been the foundation of a European Defence Community, whereby the military resources of the six ECSC members plus Britain would be integrated into a single structure for common defence; political union would then have been a short step away. However the British refused to participate and in 1954 EDC was killed off by the French National Assembly suspicious of a rearmed Germany and, as a major colonial power, reluctant to compromise their freedom of action. In 1955 the Brussels Treaty, which had been a precursor for NATO, was extended to include Germany and Italy under the umbrella of a new organization, the Western European Union (WEU), but its operational responsibilities had been transferred to NATO and it became dormant. The Atlantic Alliance remained the linchpin of European defence throughout the Cold War and the ensuing period of detente; WEU was reactivated in 1986 and is now being developed as the European pillar of NATO.[2]

Once it had been established that defence was not to be the common purpose driving European integration, attention shifted from politics to economics and trade. Nationalism had proved to be the godfather to protection; the national market was reserved for national producers creating domestic jobs and could be extended by annexation or trade treaty when additional outlets were needed to sustain growth. The need to extend national markets had been an underlying cause of both World Wars. The creation of a customs union between the Six and thus free trade between them would act as an effective antidote to nationalism and, as mutual interdependence increased, the process of integration would become irreversible. An historical precedent lay to hand in the shape of the *Zollverein* which had been the precursor of the unified Germany; a European common market seemed the obvious counter to the overwhelming economic dominance of the United States. The Messina Conference was summoned to establish a Customs Union and, building on the experience of the ECSC, design the supranational structure that would hold it together.

Britain sent an observer to the Messina Conference but he was quickly withdrawn and the UK Government took no part in the negotiations.[3] Given the attitude prevailing at the time this was hardly surprising. Britain was the only European country that had neither been defeated nor occupied during the war, and there was reason to believe that she could continue to play a big power role in partnership with the United States. World-wide influence could be exercised through the Commonwealth and Britain's permanent membership of the UN Security Council; there was no need to become ensnared in dubious Continental entanglements which had little chance of success. These post-imperial pretensions were finally buried in the sands of Suez, but by then it was too late; the basic architecture of the European Community had been agreed and was already being put in place.

Britain's absence from the negotiating table meant that France was the dominant influence in the negotiations at Messina, the partner that had to be satisfied above all if the project was to get off the ground. As a result, the ethos of the Community acquired a marked French bias which survives to this day, both in its constitutional architecture and the culture of its institutions. The spirit of protection, which is heavily entrenched in French political thinking, is evident in the Common Agricultural Policy (CAP) and the many references to Community Preference, and bureaucratic centralism, which has been the hallmark of French administration since the days of Richelieu, is characteristic of the mind-set of the European

Commission. French remains the natural language of European civil servants in the Commission and the Council and Parliament's secretariats, leaving the Anglo-Saxons with a nagging feeling that they are out in the cold. British scepticism about the goals of European Union is not simply a product of history: it owes much to the feeling that the Union is an alien body with which they can never be comfortable.[4]

The EEC Treaty took over the institutions which had been established for the ECSC and their functions were merged. Thus the ECSC High Authority became the European Commission; the Special Council, the Council of Ministers; the Common Assembly, the European Parliament; the Court of Justice, the European Court of Justice. These institutions will be examined in detail in subsequent chapters, but it is important to start with a general idea of the structure.

The European Commission was intended by the Founding Fathers to be the embryo of an eventual European Government. It is a college, a collective body, composed of individuals who are nominated by their national governments, but appointed by the Council as a whole. They are required by Article 157 of the Treaty to be completely independent in the performance of their duties and neither seek nor take instructions from any government. Its first president, the German Walter Hallstein, described its role as follows:

> The Commission's task is to safeguard the Community interest. It is the mainspring of the Community for it alone can initiate legislation. It mediates between the Community and the particular interests of the member states – and not only in the final phase of the decision-making process in the Council.[5]

As Guardian of the Treaties the Commission is responsible for ensuring that they are properly applied; it has the sole right to initiate legislation which is required by or consistent with the Treaty; it has an autonomous right of decision and is equal in status with the Council of Ministers. It is in no sense a Council secretariat or subordinate body.

If the Commission is the Executive, the Council of Ministers, which is also a collegiate body, is the legislature with power to act on Commission proposals. Article 155 clearly envisages that additional powers will be conferred on the Commission by the

Council, so that it would gradually take over more powers from the states. The Council was intended to provide the mechanism whereby powers could be devolved to the Commission following agreement between the states; for example by a single Regulation in 1965 the Council transferred responsibility for competition policy to the Commission, which has retained complete autonomy in this area ever since. Such a wholesale transfer of competence would be unthinkable today.[6]

The institutional history of the European Community has been dominated by the tension which exists between its leading institutions. The Council, on which the governments are represented, has been increasingly reluctant to cede power to the Commission now that the original tide of integrationist euphoria has receded. Through the Committee of Permanent Representatives (COREPER) the Council has developed a network of specialist working groups, composed of national civil servants, where Commission proposals are brokered and frequently watered down; COREPER itself has assumed the responsibility for the final clearance of legislation for approval by Ministers. Where the Council cannot agree the proposal will normally be referred back to the Permanent Representatives for further consideration.

The power of the Council has been further strengthened by the establishment of legislative Committees charged with the implementation of framework legislation and the oversight of the structural funds and other Community programmes. The constitution and powers of these Committees, usually referred to as comitology, are among the most arcane processes of government and since, like the Council itself, they meet in secret, their decision-making is shrouded in mystery and wholly unchecked by any kind of democratic accountability. It is ironic that when individual Ministers and commentators rail at 'Brussels' as the embodiment of bureaucratic interference, they are really attacking their own national officials who make deals to reflect an administrative consensus in a manner that few of the responsible Ministers understand. The Commission has substantial influence on this process, but there is no doubt where real power lies.

In the original Treaty the European Parliament, originally styled the Assembly, was required to meet in an annual session beginning on the second Tuesday in March. It was to receive and debate the Commission's annual report; under Article 144 it had the power to force the Commission to resign; and it had the right to receive oral or written replies to questions to the Commission. Various other provisions require the Council to ask the opinion of the Assembly before adopting legislation, but its only right of initiative was to prepare proposals for a uniform system of election by direct universal suffrage. Although the European Parliament has materially increased its power and influence since the Treaty was signed, it has never succeeded in mustering the necessary majority to dismiss the Commission nor, despite several attempts, has it been able to agree a proposal for a uniform electoral system.

The constitution of the European Parliament as it is now known reflects the Continental attitude to elected chambers rather than that which prevails in Britain, where the Crown in Parliament is the supreme organ of the state and the embodiment of the national will. In most Continental countries the Assembly has a supervisory role in the legislative process: it legitimizes the Government's programme on behalf of the citizens. It is not for the most part expected to play an active role in shaping legislation; that is the responsibility of the executive. Typically parliaments in Europe will approve a government's programme with a vote of confidence and endorse the national budget. Thereafter their role is to monitor implementation, but they are not expected to get pro-actively involved in the process of government itself.

This seems to be the role envisaged for the Assembly by the original treaties, and goes some way to explaining why, in Britain at least, the European Parliament has never succeeded in capturing the public imagination and therefore commanding the popular esteem and support that is enjoyed by the House of Commons. Its success in extending its role is rooted in the perception of both Council and Commission that it needs more powers if it is to provide the democratic legitimacy which the Community so clearly needs; accordingly they have been prepared to sacrifice administrative convenience in the interests of public acceptability. As a result the Parliament has become the creature of its sister institutions rather than the body that calls them to account. There is no question that the European Parliament's failure to establish itself has given rise to a democratic deficit. Individual ministers are responsible to their national parliaments for their actions, but the Council of Ministers, acting as a collegiate body, is answerable to none; indeed since meetings of the Council are held in secret, MPs cannot be sure how their particular Minister may have acted so their influence is extremely limited. Federalists have argued that this lack of accountability can only be compensated by increased powers for the European Parliament, which should be placed on an equal footing with the Council; Eurosceptics have claimed that the only way of preserving parliamentary accountability is to repatriate powers from the European Community to the national governments. Neither solution is particularly satisfactory, but until some way is found of opening the Council to detailed parliamentary scrutiny, possibly by associating national parliaments more closely with the legislative process, the democratic credentials of the Community will be vulnerable to attack.[7]

The European Court of Justice (ECJ) was established 'to ensure that in the interpretation and application of this Treaty the law is observed.'[8] As such it can hear suits brought by the Commission against member states and by member states and the institutions themselves against the Council and Commission if they fail to carry out their obligations under the Treaties. The ECJ is a continental style supreme court, the final arbiter and interpreter of a written constitution. As the Community has developed the Court has made increasing use of its powers of interpretation to extend the bounds of Community competence. In so doing the judges can fairly claim to be fulfilling the intention of the Treaties, though British jurists would argue that this is a matter for elected parliaments, not nominated judges.

These four autonomous institutions embody the European Community, as established by the Treaty of Rome. As Professor Henig has pointed out, it is a quasi-federal structure, in so far as competences have been allocated to different levels of government according to a framework established by treaty; within that framework each institution has autonomous rights and obligations. It is not a true federation since ultimate power remains with the member states, who retain the right to secede.

The concept of a single institutional structure to manage Community policies and promote the cause of European Union was implicit in the Treaty of Rome and stated clearly in the preamble to the 1965 Merger Treaty.[9] The Treaty of European

Union (TEU), which was concluded at Maastricht and came into force in November 1992, introduced an entirely new concept whereby the new European Union was composed of three independent pillars, linked together through the European Council of Heads of State and Government which was the ultimate authority in each case. The activities of the autonomous institutions, Council, Commission, Parliament and Court of Justice, established by the Treaty of Rome with its elaborate arrangement of interlocking rights and obligations, were confined to the first pillar, that is the European Community, as it emerged from the Single European Act. The two other pillars, Common Foreign and Security Policy and Justice and Home Affairs, had a different and separate structure. The Council remained the decision-making body, but the Commission has no exclusive right of initiative and was merely entitled to participate in Council meetings. The Parliament has a right to be consulted and informed but no legislative role, while the Court of Justice has no jurisdiction whatever, so that these two pillars are outside the ambit of Community law. This arrangement for the second and third pillars is entirely intergovernmental, reminiscent of other international organizations such as the United Nations, and the North Atlantic Alliance, having little in common with the quasi-federal structure of the European Community proper. In this way Maastricht was indeed a triumph for intergovernmentalism, a turning point at which it became clear that the original aspiration for a federal system of government for Europe with independent supranational institutions was not going to be realized.

Much of the debate in Britain about federalism is misconceived. The federal character of the Community is explicit in the Treaties and has been affirmed in numerous declarations, but it is not a federal state in the sense of the United States or even a confederation such as Switzerland, though it could develop in that direction. The real issue is the division of competences between the supranational institutions and the member states. The Founding Fathers, who were of course members of national governments, intended that the Community should be driven by an elite central bureaucracy which would provide the dynamic for closer integration; in their view this was the best way to bring Europeans together in peace and prosperity. Since that time their successors have become increasingly reluctant to agree to the further transfers of power that would be necessary for European government to become a reality; the history of the European Community is one of continuous tension between the national and the collective interest as member states 'fight their corner'. Within the Community itself this tension is reflected in the constant struggle for institutional supremacy between Council and Commission.

The insight that makes the European Community unique among multinational organizations is that it has an independent system of law administered by a supranational Court and Commission. If national interests are to be subordinated to the collective, there has to be an autonomous supranational element in the structure to make sure that the collective interest is sustained and that the member states respect the commitments into which they have entered. Those states that join have implicitly accepted that their national interests will be best protected by their acting together rather than separately, even if this means making sacrifices in the short term. For example fish stocks need to be preserved if a European fishing industry is to survive and this can only be achieved by cooperation between the coastal states. Such cooperation necessarily involves the sacrifice of some short-term national interests, with painful consequences for some fishermen who feel they are being deprived of their prerogative to catch as many fish as they like in their own waters. The alternative would be a free-for-all with the risk of conflict between neighbours and the probable destruction of the fish stocks that the fishermen themselves need to survive. In other words the national interest is best protected by sacrificing short-term advantage to medium-term good. It is difficult for national governments to explain this to their own embattled fishermen who are primarily concerned with survival in the short term, so the supranational institutions are called in aid to provide an alibi and prevent the national governments from succumbing to public pressure and abandoning the Common Fisheries Policy. Acceptance by the partners of the paramountcy and binding nature of European law is fundamental to the Community system, and attempts to undermine it threaten the existence of the EC as we know it.

Just because the Community is required to prevent its members from breaking agreements or taking short-term action to satisfy domestic pressure groups, it is an easy target for those who believe in the supremacy of the nation-state. Moreover the national bureaucracies understandably resent any concession of their powers to the centre and are suspicious of the ambitions of the supranational Commission. The temptation to blame alien bureaucrats for unpopular decisions that have actually been taken by the domestic administration is very strong. These pressures, coupled with the lack of an independent political base, have dimmed the original vision of a United Europe and blunted the federalist dynamic. Having made the original commitment to an 'Ever Closer Union' by signing the Treaty of Rome, governments both individually and through the Council, have sought to put limits round the authority of the supranational institutions and even claw back some of the powers that had been rashly conceded in earlier times. Having willed the end they have regularly recoiled from accepting the means.

Whereas national bureaucrats have been instinctively hostile to the acquisition of power by Brussels, public policy has differed between the member states. By and large the smaller countries such as Denmark and the Benelux have seen the Community as a guarantee against domination by their larger neighbours; Italy, Spain and the poorer countries of the south have seen it as a way of catching up with their more economically advanced competitors. For France it has been a vehicle for pursuing national ambitions, while for Germany it is the means of assuaging the guilt of having been responsible for two world wars. While these governments may have chafed at many of the inconveniences of Community life, they have remained committed to its progressive development. By contrast Britain's insularity, historically stable institutions and lingering memories of a glorious past has made her an unwilling and half-hearted convert to the European ideal; public opinion has seldom been more than lukewarm. It was Britain's detachment that nearly caused the Community to be still-born in the first place and British scepticism has been at the heart of the resistance to federalist ambitions since she joined belatedly in 1973.

In Community terms the federal question might be expressed as follows: 'What are the appropriate competences necessary for the federal institutions to exercise for the Community to be held together as an economic and political unit?' Article 3b of the Treaty of European Union which was negotiated at Maastricht provides an answer in the concept of subsidiarity.

'The Community shall take action . . . only if and in so far as the objectives of the proposed action cannot be sufficiently achieved by the Member States and therefore by reason of the scale and effects of the proposed action, be better achieved by the Community.'

This minimalism is a long way from the language and intention of the original Treaty which was drafted at a time when the presumption was in favour of unity and common action. Taken together with the intergovernmental pillars introduced at Maastricht, which limit the role of the Commission and Parliament in the important new policy areas of Common Foreign and Security Policy and Justice and Home Affairs, and excludes them entirely from the jurisdiction of the European Court, Article 3b is evidence of how far the federal tide has ebbed since the heady days of the early sixties. The fact is that, good intentions notwithstanding, the Community has remained the product of an elitist governing class and has never put down roots in the affections and esteem of its citizens. In the 1980s Altiero Spinelli's courageous attempts to sell his federalist ideal to the people over the heads of national governments ended in failure; the European Parliament has not succeeded in establishing itself as a credible representative of the popular will. For all the vision and passion of those who believe in a federal union, the citizens of Europe remain to be convinced.

Generally speaking the European Community has functioned well and made rapid progress when there has been an identifiable common purpose reflecting widespread popular consent. When these elements are lacking it has been uncertain and ineffective, a prey to the contradictions that are inherent in its structure. Its history has been one of bouts of rapid progress interspersed with periods of inertia and decline. In subsequent chapters we shall look at the role of the institutions against the background of recent history and demonstrate the extent to which the federal ideals of the Founding Fathers have been undermined by the realities of conflicting interests, internally between the institutions themselves, and externally between the member states.

In the middle 1990s major questions hover over the future of the European Union as its members grapple with the consequences of technological advance and global interdependence. Assumptions that may have seemed obvious in the post-war period are no longer easily accepted, as governments struggle to meet the rapidly rising expectations of their electorates. As the free democracies of Western Europe contemplate an uncertain future, it is worth reminding ourselves that the European Union came into being because of its founders' first-hand experience of the destructive potential of unbridled nationalism. The ethnic conflicts in former Yugoslavia and parts of the former Soviet Union are timely reminders of the horrors that ensue when international order breaks down and nationalist instincts are allowed free reign. If the European Union were to fail, the alternative would be the balkanization of Western Europe, an end to stability and the prosperity and living standards which we have come to take for granted. With its contradictions and internal tensions the European Union is far from the model of co-operation under the rule of law that was originally envisaged, but it remains the main bulwark against a modern form of barbarism which could destroy our civilization for ever. Whatever we may think about the 'Ever Closer Union' we all have a vested interest that it should succeed.

2 The European Commission: Government by bureaucrat?

When British politicians and journalists complain about 'Brussels' they are usually thinking of the European Commission, that mysterious and powerful collection of non-elected bureaucrats whose decisions are reputed to have a substantial impact on our daily lives and are accountable to no one for their actions. The myth of the power-crazed bureaucrats, bent on the creation of a centralized superstate, has a special potency for the British press; Christopher Booker, who has made a considerable name for himself as a critic of everything to do with the European Union wrote in a *Sunday Telegraph* article:

> One of the more insidious things about the way the influence of the EC now seeps up like a dank fog through every nook and cranny of British life is the way in which it is so often obscured.[1]

He went on to attack the Commission for its part in ending the Milk Marketing Board's monopoly as a means of introducing more competition into the system for distributing milk. The phrase 'nooks and crannies' is not original, it was first used by Douglas Hurd, normally regarded as a pro-European, in his speech to the 1991 Conservative Party Conference which shows how even those who support Britain's membership of the EU are obsessed by the image of the meddling bureaucrat.

Part of the problem lies in the fact that the Commission is a political hybrid which does not fit easily into the British tradition which distinguishes Ministers from non-elected civil servants. The commissioners themselves are politicians and have a political role, but they are appointed by their national governments and although they can be dismissed en bloc by the European Parliament, they are individually accountable to no one.

The services over which they preside are staffed by permanent officials who, thanks to a permissive staff regulation are virtually irremovable, and appear totally detached from the everyday life of the citizen, yet have the power to initiate legislation which materially affects the way we live and do business. Matters are not helped by the sense of Olympian superiority that characterizes the Commission's self image and its impenetrable multilingual jargon which prevents it from explaining its actions in terms the ordinary person can understand.

As we have seen, the Commission was conceived by Jean Monnet and his collaborators as the embryo of a European Government. Article 155 of the Treaty of Rome sets out its responsibilities as follows:

> In order to ensure the proper functioning and development of the Common Market, the Commission shall:
> — ensure the provisions of this Treaty and the measures taken by the institutions pursuant thereto are applied;
> — formulate recommendations or deliver opinions on matters that are dealt with in this Treaty, if it expressly so provides or if the Commission considers it necessary;
> — have its own power of decision and participate in the shaping of measures taken by the Council and by the Assembly in the manner provided for in this Treaty;
> — exercise the powers conferred on it by the Council for the implementation of the rules laid down by the latter.

The Commission is the Guardian of the Treaties, responsible for ensuring that the member states carry out their obligations, and it has the right to initiate proposals for legislation, provided that it can find a legal base within the Treaty for so doing. It is an autonomous partner with a specific role in the legislative process and may exercise additional powers or competences if they are conferred by the Council. Indeed it may initiate extensions to its own powers by invoking Article 235:

> If action by the Community should prove necessary to attain in the course of the operation of the common market, one of the objectives of the Community and this Treaty has not provided the necessary powers, the Council shall, acting unanimously on a proposal from the Commission and after consulting the Assembly, take the appropriate measures.

The powers of the Commission reflect the traditional French attachment to a strong central executive staffed by elite public servants whose high-mindedness compensates for the vagaries of elected politicians.

The history of the Community is in many respects the story of a continuing struggle between the collective interest represented by the supranational Commission and states' rights which are defended by the Council of Ministers and the member states themselves. Between 1957 when the Treaty of Rome was signed and 1965 there was a period of rapid growth in the Commission's authority under its first president, the German Walter Hallstein. The principal achievement of this period was the creation of the Common Agricultural Policy (CAP), which embodied the essential bargain between France and Germany: a common market for agricultural products underpinned by border controls and uniform prices to suit France, in return for a free trade in industrial goods and reductions of customs tariffs which were merged in a single system to accommodate the Germans. This was finally concluded after arduous negotiations, with an agreement on common prices brokered by the Dutch Commissioner, Sicco Mansholt, in December 1964.

The Commission then launched an initiative based on Article 201 of the Treaty, proposing that the Community budget would in future be funded by a system of 'Own Resources' rather than direct contributions from the member states. Under this system income from customs duties under the Common External Tariff (CET) and agricultural levies flowing from the CAP would belong to the Community as of right, giving it a degree of financial independence from the member states. This was a step too far for President de Gaulle who had become increasingly wary of the Commission's pretensions; the French, who held the Presidency of the Council, blocked the adoption of the Own Resources decision and then, on 30 June 1965, withdrew their representatives from all Community bodies when the Council failed to agree measures to finance the CAP by direct contributions to the EC budget.

Remarkably the Community held together, thanks to a close alliance between the Commission and the German Foreign Minister Gerhard Schroeder. Business continued normally despite the French 'empty chair' and the crisis was resolved when they ended their boycott in February 1966, and the financial regulation establishing the Own Resources system was agreed in

May.[2] The French were mollified by a note included in the Council minutes stating that: 'France considers that when important issues are at stake discussion must be continued until unanimous agreement is reached.'

This became known as the Luxembourg Compromise and was used for some years to justify the retention of majority voting in the Council even when the Treaty provided otherwise. Successive presidencies refused to put issues to vote in the Council as long as any one member state was opposed, so unanimity became the rule. The national veto was highly prized by the British, and was regularly cited by Margaret Thatcher as proof that national sovereignty remained intact. The threat to use the veto was an important bargaining chip in negotiations over the British budget contribution, but equally it enabled other member states to delay the passage of legislation to create a common market in financial services and other areas where the British wanted progress to be made. For all the mythology that grew up around the Luxembourg Compromise, it was never more than a note in the minutes recording the opinion of one member state and fell into disuse after the Council successfully over-rode an attempted British veto on the 1982 agricultural price settlement. By that time it had become clear that the requirement for unanimity had become a barrier to further progress in economic integration.

The 1965 crisis was a major turning point in so far as it enabled the Commission to consolidate its position as an independent institution in its own right. Its room for manoeuvre was increased by the implementation of the Own Resources decision and its self confidence boosted by its demonstrating that the collective will for closer integration was sufficiently strong to face down the most nationalist of the member states. De Gaulle's attitude to the Community was not popular in France: his intransigence over Europe contributed to his relatively poor showing in the presidential elections in the autumn of 1965 and this had been a factor in his decision to back down and resolve the crisis. Since this episode neither Mrs Thatcher nor any other national leader has attempted this kind of brinkmanship and for the next 37 years, until the Danish 'No' vote in their 1992 referendum, it was generally assumed that public opinion had accepted the idea of closer European union and that therefore no single government could take on the rest of the Community and win.

Following the conclusion of the Merger Treaty April 1965, the EC, ECSC and the treaty establishing the European Atomic Energy Community (EURATOM) were brought together into a single institutional structure. The remainder of the decade was taken up with the consolidation of progress achieved during the Hallstein presidency with the implementation of the CAP and the Own Resources system. This was a period during which the Commission steadily extended its competences, notably through Regulation 17/67 by which, in a rare example of the Monnet system working as intended, the Council transferred total responsibility for the administration of competition policy to the Commission, which is accountable only to the Court of Justice for its actions in this policy area.

In 1970 a Conservative government was returned to power in the United Kingdom and, under the leadership of Edward Heath, was able to conclude the negotiations for British Accession. This brought to an end the long saga of Britain's application to join the European Community, launched by Harold Macmillan in 1961, blocked in the debacle of de Gaulle's '*Non*' in 1963, relaunched by Harold Wilson and George Brown, only to run into a second '*Non*' in 1968. Britain, accompanied by Denmark and Ireland, joined the Community on 1 January 1973, an enlargement scarcely affected by Norway's negative vote in a national referendum. Throughout the period of the accession negotiations, British entry had been staunchly supported by the Dutch and their Benelux associates who saw the United Kingdom as a natural counterbalance to Franco-German dominance. They were quickly disillusioned. Success in the negotiations was the result of a remarkable personal rapport between Edward Heath and Georges Pompidou, de Gaulle's successor as President of France. Faced with the oil shocks following the Yom Kippur War of 1973, Britain was unprepared to share her North Sea oil reserves with her partners and showed no signs of taking a *communautaire* line in the Council. The Labour Opposition, which had opposed the Accession Treaty, refused to nominate a delegation to the European Parliament.

The first European Council of Heads of State and Government, convened by President Giscard d'Estaing in June 1973, adopted the Werner Report which looked forward to Economic and Monetary Union (EMU) by the end of the decade and commissioned a report by Leo Tindemans, Prime Minister of Belgium, on the mechanics of a political union to parallel increasing economic integration. Applications from Spain, Greece and Portugal to join were referred to the Commission for an opinion; in retrospect the summer of 1973 marks the conclusion of a period when progress towards a European Union seemed increasingly assured.

The Yom Kippur War which broke out in October 1973 and the successive oil shocks which followed delivered a sharp check to European growth rates and with it confidence in European solutions to the economic problems of the individual member states. The European Council under the dual leadership of President Giscard d'Estaing and Chancellor Helmut Schmidt began to assert itself, and a series of weak presidencies saw the Commission marking time. In particular the attachment of the Council to unanimity in the name of the Luxembourg Compromise paralysed decision-making, and Commission initiatives such as the Fifth Company Law Directive which would have introduced a common European Company Statute with mandatory trade union representation on supervisory boards were irretrievably blocked. The Commission continued to propose immensely detailed legislation on matters such as common standards and the mutual recognition of qualifications which made no progress in the face of increasing obstruction by the member states who were less and less willing to make concessions on grounds of Community interest. The conclusion of a Common Fisheries Policy, which was foreseen as a priority in the Treaty, made no progress in the face of Danish intransigence and it took 17 years to agree a directive on the mutual recognition of the qualifications of architects. The quest for unanimity had a paralysing effect on the legislative process as the member states had no excuse for compromise and the Commission's role as honest broker was diminished as its lack of effectiveness was revealed.

The launch of the European Monetary System in 1978 and the first direct elections to the European Parliament in June 1979 disguised the underlying malaise. The Own Resources system was increasingly under strain from exploding agricultural expenditure and the Thorn presidency, 1980–84, was destroyed by internecine warfare between the member states over the British budget contribution. Greece acceded to the

Community in 1983, but negotiations with Spain and Portugal were hopelessly stalled as the Community fought to resolve the the deadlock over increasing the budget ceiling. In 1984 the US Secretary for Commerce, Malcolm Baldridge, speaking in Venice, described the phenomenon of Euro-sclerosis, a condition of labour market rigidities and resistance to change which was steadily eroding competitiveness with the US, Japan, and the economies of the Pacific rim. The Community was enjoying a standard of living way beyond its means and was incapable of taking the decisions necessary to deal with its problems. Although the Customs Union had finally been achieved in 1980, fulfilling one of the main objectives of the Treaty of Rome, non-tariff barriers to trade were an increasingly effective means of national protection and the ideal of a common market remained as far away as ever. Attempts by the British Presidency of 1983 to liberalize the market for insurance and other financial services failed to get off the ground and this helped to convince the Thatcher Government that unanimity was an insuperable barrier to progress in establishing a 'real Common Market'.

Jacques Delors, who as President Mitterrand's Minister of Finance had been responsible for reversing the inflationary programme on which the Socialists had fought the 1981 election, became President of the Commission in January 1985. A Catholic Socialist with a messianic belief in the *Vocation Européen*, he reinvigorated the Commission with the spirit of the French *haute administration* and restored its institutional self-belief. In partnership with the new British Commissioner, Arthur Cockfield, he launched a White Paper listing 300 directives necessary to strip away non-tariff barriers and create a true common market based on four basic freedoms of movement – goods, people, capital and services – and undertook to complete the programme by 1992, an eight-year period encompassing the term of office of two Commissions. After a series of grinding negotiations he finally reached agreement with Margaret Thatcher on a rebate to redress the imbalance in the British contribution to the EC budget in 1986 and as a result revamped the Own Resources system to create some budgetary headroom. Negotiations for the accession of Spain and Portugal were finally completed on the back of this settlement and they joined the Community on 1 January 1987: the Ten became the Twelve. When Delors was reappointed President of the Commission in

1989 the Community had received a new lease of life and the Euro-sclerosis identified by Baldridge seemed buried in the past. By any test it was a remarkable personal achievement and Jacques Delors deserves to be ranked alongside Jean Monnet and Walter Hallstein as one of the principal architects of the European Union.

The central achievement of the first Delors presidency was the Intergovernmental Conference of 1986 which produced the Single European Act. This was a series of amendments to the original Treaty of Rome which set a date for completion of the single market and by introducing majority voting in the Council for all those measures specified in the Cockfield White Paper, made it possible to tackle non-tariff barriers to trade and establish a system of mutually recognized standards. The key provisions are Article 8a which states:

> The Community shall adopt measures with the aim of progressively establishing the internal market over a period expiring on 31st December 1992 . . .
>
> The internal market shall comprise an area without internal frontiers in which the freedom of movement of goods, persons, services and capital is ensured in accordance with the provisions of this Treaty.

and Article 100a which states:

> . . . The Council shall, acting by a qualified majority on a proposal from the Commission in co-operation with the European Parliament and after consulting the Economic and Social Committee, adopt measures for the approximation of the provisions laid down by law, regulation or administrative action which have as their object the establishment and functioning of the internal market.

A qualified majority was defined in Article 148 as 54 out of a possible 76 votes. France, Germany, Italy and the UK had ten votes each, Spain eight, Belgium, Greece, Holland and Portugal five, Denmark and Ireland three and Luxembourg two. A blocking minority of 22 could be achieved by two big member states and one small one, or one big state and three small ones other than Luxembourg. The principle of unanimity and the alleged effect of the Luxembourg Compromise seemed finally to have been laid to rest.

These provisions which made the achievement of the single market possible were accepted by the member states without any of the Parliamentary shenanigans and referenda crises which were to accompany the ratification of the Treaty of Maastricht in 1992. Prompted by Margaret Thatcher, the Heads of Government believed that the establishment of a 'real common market' was an essential element in securing economic recovery and that this could not be delivered if a national veto was available. They were prepared to turn a blind eye to the implications for national sovereignty in pursuit of an overriding national interest. It was the special genius of Jacques Delors that he was able to identify the essential goal of economic growth which provided the common purpose necessary to suppress the national hesitations of the member states.

Before the Single European Act, harmonization had been seen as a necessary condition for the free movement of goods. If a product or service was to cross national frontiers unimpeded, there had to be a single set of European standards based on common definitions which would override domestic standards, and thus prevent the erection of non-tariff barriers to trade. The result was a series of immensely detailed proposals which proved quite impossible to carry through a Council where the requirement for unanimity prevailed, with the result that they remained blocked for years. The failure to carry through the harmonization programme was an important factor in Euro-sclerosis, as the market remained fragmented with all manner of controls on the free movement of goods.

The senior British Commissioner, Lord Cockfield, drafted the 1985 White Paper which described the nature of the single market and identified the measures necessary to achieve it. Cockfield devised the so-called 'New Approach' by which, instead of proposals which sought to legislate in detail for all conceivable situations, the Commission drafted framework directives which established general principles, leaving the detailed implementation to national authorities or independent European standard-setting bodies. In so doing he built on the jurisprudence of the Court of Justice which established the principle of mutual recognition, that is a standard or qualification recognized by a particular national authority must normally be accepted by all the others.[3]

During the late seventies and early eighties the Commission, which was broadly left of centre in its political bias, made a series of proposals for Directives which were designed to harmonise social and labour market legislation across the Community. These included the Fifth Company Law Directive, which would have introduced the German system of two-tier boards with the Supervisory Board containing equal numbers of trade union and shareholder nominees, directives on part-time and temporary work, parental leave and most notoriously the Vredeling Directive called after the Dutch Socialist Commissioner, Henk Vredeling. This sought to make consultation with trade unions at a European level mandatory before major decisions, such as sale of a plant, alteration of activity or closure, were taken in respect of subsidiaries by transnational corporations. The legal base for these proposals was Article 100, which provided that:

> The Council shall, acting unanimously on a proposal from the Commission, issue directives for the approximation of such provisions laid down by law, regulation or administrative action in Member States as directly affect the establishment of the common market.

The Commission, with the active support of the trade unions, took the view that common provisions for the labour market were an essential feature of the single market; in their absence multinational companies would take advantage of countries with lower levels of social protection and invest in them, rather than suffer the burdens of the more developed social systems in Germany and the Benelux countries. This practice, known as social dumping, was seen as a major threat to the completion of the single market.

Much to the frustration of the trade unions, the unanimity requirement had enabled Britain to block these social engineering directives with the connivance of some of the southern states, which feared the erosion of this aspect of their comparative advantage. Jacques Delors believed that the completion of the single market would prove impossible if it did not have trade union backing; in 1985 he relaunched the Social Dialogue between UNICE,[4] representing the European employers, and the European Trade Union Confederation (ETUC) for the employees, known collectively as the social partners. He announced that the Commission would make proposals for social legislation only on the basis of agreement reached by the social partners, hoping to avoid blockages in the Council if a broad consensus between both sides of industry, through the process of 'collective bargaining at the European level', could be achieved. He believed that the momentum resulting from such a consensus would make it difficult for individual member states to block proposals in the Council.

The Single European Act recast Article 118 of the Treaty which had given the Commission a right to deliver opinions but not to introduce legislation on labour market issues. In the amended Treaty, Article 118a provided for legislation to be proposed and adopted by qualified majority if it involved improvements in the working environment or measures to promote the health and safety of workers by harmonizing working conditions. Article 118b excluded relations between management and labour from the majority voting provided for in Article 118a and merely referred to the desirability of rules based on agreement.

The social partners failed to achieve any meaningful agreements on which Article 118b legislation could be based and the social engineering directives remained blocked. Following the adoption of the Single Act, the Commission widened the definition of health and safety and used Article 118a to introduce a series of directives on working hours, maternity leave and part-time work though not the mandatory consultation proposed in the Vredeling Directive. Much to the fury of the British Government a list of approximately 40 measures was published in the so-called Social Charter, adopted by a majority of the European Council at the end of 1988. The UK voted against. Relations between Margaret Thatcher and Jacques Delors, which had been relatively cordial during the renegotiation of the British budget contribution, deteriorated sharply when the President of the Commission addressed a rapturous TUC Conference in September 1987 and announced that the Single European Act had paved the way for the harmonization of working conditions throughout the single market.

Mrs Thatcher was to describe this as 'Socialism by the back Delors'.[5] The British Prime Minister felt that the Commission had reneged on a tacit agreement to confine legislation concerning the labour market to Article 118b, which required unanimity and was thus subject to a veto, while applying a strict definition of health and safety to proposals based on Article 118a which permitted majority voting. This apparent betrayal, coupled with a moment of unguarded triumphalism when Delors told the European Parliament that within ten years the bulk of social and economic legislation in Europe would be introduced at Community level,[6] convinced Mrs Thatcher that the Commission did indeed intend to establish a federal super-state and had to be resisted at all costs. These fears found their expression in the celebrated Bruges speech in September 1988 in which she called for a Community founded on 'willing and active co-operation between independent sovereign states' and lambasted the centralizing tendencies of 'Brussels'.

At the same time the speech to the TUC marked the turning point in a process by which the Labour opposition retreated from the commitment to withdraw from the EC in its 1983 election manifesto and became increasingly Euro-enthusiastic. The sea change is symbolized by Neil Kinnock's personal progression from saying 'I want out of the Common Market', in 1983, to becoming one of Britain's two Commissioners in 1995.

The end of the first Delors Presidency is a convenient point at which to take stock of this overweening bureaucracy that, as far as Margaret Thatcher was concerned, threatened the very existence of the nation-state.

The Commission employs approximately 14 000 permanent officials of whom a third are engaged in translation and interpretation into the eleven official languages. The head-count is comparable with a medium-sized County Council. At its head are the 20 commissioners who meet weekly and act collegially. Decisions are taken by vote and the majority is binding. Individual commissioners do not publicly attack Commission decisions even when they disagree with them, nor do they take instructions from their national member states. However in practice commissioners remain in close touch with their national governments and are expected to explain their likely reactions and the probable attitude of the political parties and public opinion in general to Commission proposals. Some commissioners unashamedly act as spokesmen for national interests and this is reflected throughout the institution; an Italian is no less Italian, nor a Greek less Greek because they are international civil servants. The College of Commissioners lies at the heart of the Community process whereby consensus is drawn from conflicting national interests by identifying areas where collective action can deliver a unifying common goal.

Each commissioner is supported by a cabinet, or private office, staffed by his personal appointees. These will be mostly nationals of his own member state, though usually at least one non-national is included. Cabinet members will cover different areas of interest and liaise on his behalf with their opposite numbers in the other cabinets on matters in which their commissioner has a particular interest, and act as channels of communication with the Services that report to him direct. They also keep in touch with the national governments through the Permanent Representations in Brussels. The *chefs de cabinet* meet weekly to prepare full Commission meetings and are responsible for reconciling potential differences between commissioners in advance. Under Jacques Delors' formidable *chef de cabinet*, Pascal Lamy, this meeting has assumed great importance as the forum in which the basic policy decisions are taken. Cabinet members may be selected from within the Commission services or be seconded by national governments; when a commissioner's five-year term of office expires, members of his cabinet are often placed in senior positions in the Services, a practice known as parachuting and much resented by permanent officials.

The Commission's Services, as the permanent departments are known, are organized into 23 directorates general covering specific policy areas. There are also a number of free-standing ad hoc services and task forces which are set up for particular purposes. The directors general, who are roughly equivalent to permanent under-secretaries, report to individual commissioners who supervise portfolios of two or more Services. Convention dictates that a director general may not be of the same nationality as his commissioner, and holders of these key posts, which are much sought after by the member states acting through their Permanent Representations, have to reflect a balance of nationality. Directorates general are subdivided into directorates and these in turn break down into divisions, headed by a *chef de division*, which form the basic departmental unit.

Officials fall into five categories which are lettered A–E. A grades are graduates who are the equivalent of the administrative grade in the British civil service, ranks are numbered

1–7 with directors general as A1, directors and chief advisers A2, *chefs de division* A3 and so on. Category B are non-graduate entrants roughly comparable to the civil service executive grade, C is the secretarial grade and Ds and Es support services and drivers. The Translation Service has its own analogous system LA, LB etc. Entrance to the Service is by a competitive examination, known as the Concours. Candidates, who must be fluent in at least one Community language other than their own, undergo written examinations in economics and law and an oral examination on the Community and its history. Notices of competitions are published periodically in the *Official Journal* and successful applicants are placed on a reserve list from which they may be summoned when a suitable vacancy occurs. Convention dictates that the Commission services reflect an overall national balance between the member states so if a particular country is over-represented an informal freeze will operate until this is restored. The reserve list is rolled over every two to three years after which applicants have to apply to be readmitted and may be required to retake the Concours.

Thanks to an extremely favourable tax regime, European civil servants enjoy salaries somewhat in excess of those of their national counterparts, though the gap has been reduced as a result of constant pressure on the Community budget. The Staff Regulation which was introduced in the sixties provides a high degree of employment protection, so that it is almost impossible to remove an official against his will. As a result promotion, which depends on length of service and nationality as much as merit, is extremely slow, leading to a good deal of dissatisfaction in the middle ranks of the Service. This has been compounded by the tendency of member states to insist on seconding members of their home civil service to the most important posts as well as parachuting former members of cabinets. From time to time shake-outs take place to make more room for new entrants, severance terms for those who take early retirement in the interests of the Community are extremely generous and the source of many press stories about gold-plated Euro bureaucrats.

The Commission handles a considerable weight of routine secondary legislation, which implement the CAP, customs regulations and external trade agreements. Regulations in these fields where the Commission has sole competence are directly binding on the member states, a loss of national sovereignty, expressed in the equivalent of a statutory instrument. Direct- ives are general statements of principle and objectives which are binding on the member states to whom they are addressed but are implemented by secondary legislation at national level. This has led to an uneven application of EC law, although the Court of Justice has ruled that once directives are adopted their general spirit has to be respected even if the secondary legislation has not been passed.

Most primary legislation originates with a Communication from the Commission to the Council which suggests a certain course of action to deal with a particular issue and outlines the necessary instruments to achieve it. This is accepted by the Council in the form of a resolution, at which point the Service responsible will produce the first working draft. When, as is usually the case, the subject involves one or more services the draft will be considered by an interservice working group and amended as necessary. At this stage consultations with out- side interests may take place; the Commission normally pre- fers to deal with representative bodies rather than individuals or firms and there are a number of recognized advisory bodies which may be asked for an opinion. There will also be contacts with the national representations. Successive drafts will be considered by the working group until a consensus is reached and a the final version agreed by the relevant directors general. The Service whose area of responsibility is most affected will take the lead in the drafting process.

The final draft will be circulated to the cabinets and if con- troversial may be considered by the *chefs de cabinet* at their regular meeting. At any stage an individual commissioner can put a reserve on a proposal which remains blocked until he is satisfied or overridden by his colleagues. The draft instrument is finally submitted to the weekly meeting of the Commission, where it is adopted and becomes a formal proposal to the Council. Both the Council and the European Parliament can request the Commission to act or make proposals, but the Commission itself retains the sole right of initiative.

This is of course an extremely cumbersome and time- consuming process, an inevitable consequence of the wide range of interests, both political and commercial, that have to be satisfied. Because of the relatively open nature of the

Commission bureaucracy, there are frequent leaks and these give rise to many of the horror stories about meddling Brussels bureaucrats which disfigure the British press. Very often the 'nonsense' is the product of an early draft which has not yet been considered by a working group. Matters are not made any easier by the requirement that proposals be translated into 11 working languages; frequently a text which is perfectly clear in the original language version is obscure or ambivalent when translated into another. The calibre of officials varies considerably according to their background and experience and the system of promotion does not sufficiently reflect individual merit; moreover the individual officials reflect their national tradition and administrative standards, which in some cases breeds inefficiency and the occasional scandal.

Such criticisms have to be seen in the context of the scale and complexity of the enterprise: it is extremely difficult to produce legislation which can reconcile the different culture and traditions of fifteen member states and be applied fairly across the Community. National standards for animal welfare and attitudes to the enforcement of the Common Fisheries Policy are examples of cases where different national attitudes have caused widespread controversy and given rise to a feeling that the whole system is unfair.

Integration by consent can only work if the member states accept the primacy of Community legislation, and this can only happen if they feel that their essential interests are understood and respected. The Commission's ability to influence the course of events depends on its ability to provide this kind of assurance and to operate in an even-handed fashion. Whenever it appears to be pursuing its own institutional interest, suspicions are aroused and the Commission becomes the enemy rather than the impartial arbiter. Those qualities of charisma and dynamism that enabled Jacques Delors to relaunch the Community in 1985 made him vulnerable to attack for an overweening ambition to establish a European Super-State. Although such an idea was never on the cards its resonance was sufficient to make Delors and the Commission profoundly unpopular and severely weaken its authority; the idea of European government might have seemed attractive in the abstract when it was first mooted in the fifties, but the reality has proved much less palatable.

   The European Commission has not lived up to the expectations of the Founding Fathers and has conspicuously failed to
generate the public support necessary to achieve their ambitions. Although during the eighties its influence was significantly extended, this was not matched by any increase in its
powers and in spite of the conspicuous successes of the Delors
era the idea of a European government was more and more
of a mirage. In retrospect the successful facing down of de
Gaulle in 1965 marked the high water mark of Jean Monnet's
vision; ever since then, notwithstanding occasional eddies and
surges, the federalist tide has been in inexorable retreat.

3 The Council of Ministers: 'Willing co-operation between independent sovereign states'

One of the principal themes of this account of the European Union is that there is an unceasing tug of war between the quasi-federal, autonomous institutions and the member states, partners in a system, in which powers are assigned by treaty to the different organs of government. As the institution which represents the member states, the Council of Ministers is at the core of this struggle which it reflects in its internal contradictions. For instance the influence of the Council Secretariat, which has a supranational character, has been overshadowed by the prominent part played by national civil servants at Council meetings and working groups. This is typical of the institutional schizophrenia that requires the Council to act simultaneously as a single institution of the Community, embodying the collective will of the member states, and a forum for reaching intergovernmental agreements. This ambivalence and the veil of secrecy surrounding its deliberations has made the Council the most elusive of the institutions: its influence is pervasive, but it is difficult to pin down.

In spite of its contradictions the Council has been successful in increasing its power and influence far beyond the passive role envisaged for it in the Treaty of Rome, with the result that the Community has become increasingly intergovernmental in its character.

Success in the interinstitutional tussle does not mean that the Council is particularly effective at taking decisions. Agricultural policy, which is dominated by the Agricultural Council, has stubbornly resisted reform because the ministers have found it impossible to stick to their decisions in the face of opposition from their domestic agricultural lobbies. Time after time in the eighties plans to limit agricultural production were solemnly agreed, only to be unscrambled as individual ministers tried to mitigate the effects of the agreed policy on their own farmers. The annual haggle over fish quotas as each minister fights to get a good deal for his own fishermen has meant that the Common Fisheries Policy has not achieved its objective of conserving stocks. It is ironic that many of the most vociferous critics of both these policies are frequently those who advocate strengthening the role of ministers at the expense of the Commission; the record of the Council does not encourage the belief that the intergovernmental approach is the best way to carry the Community forward; indeed progress towards closer union has usually taken place at times when the Commission has played the dominant role.

Article 145 of the Treaty of Rome defined the responsibilities of the Council of Ministers as follows:

> To ensure that the objectives set out in this Treaty are attained, the Council shall in accordance with the provisions of this Treaty:
> — ensure co-ordination of the general economic policies of the Member States.
> — have power to take decisions.

Article 149 of the original Treaty weighted the balance in favour of the Commission, by requiring unanimity from the Council when amending a Commission proposal; the Commission retained the initiative by having the power to amend a proposal unilaterally up to the point at which the Council acts. This Article was repealed by the Treaty of European Union (TEU) which was concluded at Maastricht.

Thus in the original Treaty the Council was given a role that was largely passive, accepting or rejecting Commission proposals with little capacity for independent action. Its main purpose was to be the vehicle by which executive power was to be transferred to the Commission. Since 1957 its role has developed and expanded at the expense of the Commission, making it by far the most important of the institutions, certainly the Founding Fathers would never have imagined the elaborate structure of working groups and committees which have grown up over the years and have given the Council the paramount role in the legislative process.

The Council is an autonomous institution with its own rules of procedure, the senior partner in the legislative process, representing the collective will of the member states. The General Affairs Council which is composed of the Foreign Ministers, is at the apex of the structure and has overall responsibility for the Community's business. It meets every month and can be summoned on an ad hoc basis to deal with urgent matters. It is supported by a range of specialist Councils made up of departmental ministers, Agriculture, Industry, Environment, etc. which are responsible for each of these policy areas. All however meet as the Council of Ministers exercising the full competence of the institution. In recent years the Council of Economic and Finance Ministers (ECOFIN) has grown in importance and has overridden the Commission's attempts to extend its competence to fiscal and monetary policy; it frequently seems to operate as a separate institution in its own right. Major Councils such as ECOFIN, Agriculture and Industry meet monthly; others meet once formally and once informally during each six-month Presidency.

The Council Secretariat is staffed by permanent officials who are Community civil servants. They are responsible for preparing meetings and advising the Presidency and as such play a significant role in brokering agreements between national delegations. The Secretariat was recognized constitutionally for the first time in the TEU which added an additional clause to Article 151. This was a response to claims that their functions had been usurped by the teams of national civil servants who accompany their ministers to Council meetings.[1] Their primary importance lies in the continuity of their role as mediators between the national delegations, acting on behalf of the Presidency; the Secretary General of the Council is above all the man who knows where the bodies are buried.

Classically the Council acts on a proposal from the Commission after receiving the opinion of the European Parliament and in some cases the Economic and Social Committee. Policy initiatives are prepared by the Commission in the form of a Communication to the Council which sets out the broad outlines of the issue and indicates what legislation is considered necessary. The Council will discuss this and then pass a resolution setting out its reactions and inviting the Commission to produce detailed proposals. Alternatively the Council may itself take the initiative in the form of a resolution inviting the Commission to act. Once it has been formally adopted by the

Commission, the proposal is formally submitted to the Council which refers it to the European Parliament and, following an initial discussion, to one of its own working groups. These are composed of national civil servants either from the Representations or in some cases flown in especially for the purpose. The working groups study and amend Commission proposals and seek to reach a consensus, areas of disagreement are identified and boiled down to specifics to be referred to the Council proper. Ministers will discuss these issues and clarify their positions, sending the dossier back to the working groups with new guidelines for further consideration. In the days when the Council operated by unanimity this process could last for years at a time as each delegation sought to protect its national interest. Since the introduction of majority voting the Presidency continues to make every effort to achieve a consensus: only when it is clear that this cannot be achieved is the issue put to the vote. Parliamentary amendments are considered at the final stage when the Commission is asked for its opinion and the Council agrees its common position. The procedure remains cumbersome, secretive and slow.[2]

Rather as Commission meetings are prepared by *chefs de cabinet*, Council meetings are prepared by the Committee of Permanent Representatives, invariably referred to by its French acronym, COREPER, whose role is also recognized in Article 151. The heads of delegation, who are their countries' ambassadors to the European Union, work closely together and wield formidable power, performing many of the functions originally envisaged for the Secretariat. COREPER co-ordinates the activities of the council working groups, which shadow the various specialist Councils and are serviced by the Council Secretariat. It acts as the principal broker for competing national interests and its ability to establish the necessary consensus which enables the Community to act is crucial to the decision-making process.

The Council Presidency is exercised by each member state in turn for a sixth-month period. The Foreign Minister, as President in Office, presides over the General Affairs Council and his colleagues replicate this arrangement throughout the system, presiding over COREPER and the working groups. The Presidency sets the agenda for Council meetings, and so to a considerable extent the priorities of the country holding the office are reflected in Council business. The Presidency's influence is limited in that very few measures are proposed and adopted in the course of a single six-month term, and the practice has grown up of successive presidencies working together to introduce an element of continuity into the planning of Community business. Each incoming Presidency presents its programme to the European Parliament and this is followed by a general debate; a concluding report is delivered at the end of the six-month period and the head of government holding the presidency routinely makes a statement on the outcome of the European Council meeting which concludes his term of office.

The Presidency's effectiveness depends to some extent on the support it can command from its national civil service; smaller member states with limited resources find it difficult to cover the entire spectrum of responsibilities, though on the other hand they often do a better job as mediators as they have fewer axes to grind. Countries like Belgium and Luxembourg have been highly effective as they are used to the process of negotiation and compromise while others have been less successful as they have been seen to pursue their national objectives at the expense of the Community interest. Considerable prestige is attached to the Presidency and the different governments believe, rightly or wrongly, that they can enhance their standing domestically if they perform well.

The European Council of Heads of State and Government was established in 1974 and therefore not mentioned in the original Treaties: it had no institutional status before Maastricht. The idea of regular meetings of heads of government was first put forward by President Giscard d'Estaing of France and was intended to be an informal gathering to set general political directions rather than take decisions. This concept was quickly overtaken by events and the European Council became the forum for settling disputes between the governments and establishing the consensus on objectives necessary for the Community to move forward. Since the middle of the eighties the number of European Councils has been reduced from three a year to two coinciding with the end of each Council Presidency. The twice-yearly conclaves have become watersheds in the progress of the Community, at which major decisions are made on policy goals. The names of these summits have become like signposts on the route march of Community history.

In the early eighties successive summits were dominated by the need to increase the Community's own resources and the associated problem of the British budget contribution. Ever since the 1960s agriculture had absorbed the greater part of Community expenditure. This got steadily worse as the Common Agricultural Policy spiralled out of control, requiring bigger and bigger sums to support prices. As a large member state with a small agricultural sector, Britain received a disproportionately modest share of farm spending, while countries like Holland, Denmark and France with higher GDPs per capita had done relatively well. Edward Heath's attempt to compensate for this by introducing the Regional Development Fund (ERDF) in 1973 had failed, as had Harold Wilson's attempt at re-negotiation in 1975. Margaret Thatcher threatened to use her veto and succeeded in blocking the introduction of new Own Resources until she achieved a satisfactory and permanent rebate on Britain's unacceptably large net contribution. France was determined to maintain support for her farmers and Germany did not wish to become the sole paymaster. This dispute paralysed the Community for the first part of the eighties and there were a series of acrimonious summits which became famous for the British Prime Minister's use of her metaphorical handbag. A temporary settlement was reached in 1983 but fierce arguments continued until agreement was finally reached at the Fontainebleau European Council in 1986 and ratified at Brussels the following year; only then on the basis of a reformed budgetary system could the accession negotiations with Spain and Portugal get under way.

The row over the size of the budget and the scale of Britain's contribution thrust an entirely different role on the European Council making it the ultimate arbiter of Community decision-making. When the normal institutional procedures failed to deliver agreements, the Heads of Government were the only vehicle for achieving the necessary consensus. Accordingly they moved steadily closer to the mainstream of decision-making. Thus it was the Rome European Council of May 1985 that made the essential decision to adopt the single market package and convene the intergovernmental conference that produced the Single European Act; the Athens Council of 1988 took the decision to proceed with the Social Charter; and at Madrid in 1989 Margaret Thatcher was induced to agree reluctantly to the IGC on monetary union which started the process leading to Maastricht. Political union was placed on the agenda the following year at a special summit in Dublin. More recently the Edinburgh Summit in December 1992 set the seal on the Maastricht process by agreeing levels of Community spending till the end of the century, opening the door to the accession negotiations which culminated in the conclusion of agreements with Austria, Finland, Sweden and Norway.

The effect of all this has been to make the Community significantly more intergovernmental in character and this in turn has accentuated the primacy of the Council proper. It is ironic that at a time when the Commission was believed to be advancing its influence and competences through the increased use of majority voting following the Single European Act, beneath the surface the member state governments were using the Council to consolidate their supremacy.

The main instrument to be employed for this purpose was an amendment to the treaties in the Single European Act which at first sight had seemed to strengthen the Commission's role. An additional paragraph was added to Article 145 as follows:

> . . . confer on the Commission, in the acts which the Council adopts, powers for the implementation of the rules which the Council lays down. The Council may impose certain requirements in respect of the exercise of these powers. The Council may also reserve the right, in specific cases, to exercise directly implementing powers itself. The procedures referred to must be consonant with principles and rules to be laid down in advance by the Council acting unanimously on a proposal from the Commission and after obtaining the opinion of the European Parliament.

The reasoning behind this was that with a mass of extra legislation expected under the Single Market Project, there would need to be flexible procedures for detailed implementation if the process was not to become clogged and the 1992 timetable set at risk. The apparent intention was that the Council would confer wide-ranging powers on the Commission to pass implementing legislation, reserving the right to intervene in a few especially sensitive areas. The Commission duly produced a proposal which envisaged three types of statutory committee made up of representatives of the member states and chaired by a Commission representative which would consider draft implementing legislation. The different forms of Committee specified were:

> *Advisory Committee:* The Commission was bound to take its views into account, but was free to adopt its original proposal unamended.
>
> *Management Committee:* A Commission proposal could be blocked if opposed by a qualified majority.
>
> *Regulatory Committee:* A Commission proposal would fail unless it was supported by a qualified majority.

The type of Committee had to be specified in the primary legislation, which would require the opinion of the European Parliament using the co-operation procedure.

The Council Decision of 13 July 1987 substantially altered this proposal, ignoring the opinion of the European Parliament, which had sought to remove the Regulatory Committee altogether. The Decision established three Procedures corresponding to the three types of Committee proposed by the Commission, but in the case of Management and Regulatory Committees added two variants. It also introduced a new safeguard procedure to cover decisions on trade.

> *Procedure 2 (Management Committee):* If the Commission is opposed by a qualified majority in the Committee, then
> a. The Commission may delay the application of its decision for up to one month.
> b. The Commission shall delay the application of its decision for a period up to three months
>
> and, within these deadlines, the Council may, by a qualified majority take a different decision.
>
> *Procedure 3 (Regulatory Committee):* If the Commission is not supported by a qualified majority in the committee, the matter is referred to the Council which may take a decision on a Commission proposal within a deadline not exceeding three months. If it fails to adopt a decision then:
> a. The Commission shall adopt its proposal.
> b. The Commission shall adopt its proposal unless a simple majority in the Council votes against in which case no decision is taken.
>
> *Safeguard Measures:* Any member state may ask for a decision to be referred to the Council. In this case:

a. The Council has a deadline to take an alternative decision by a qualified majority.
b. The Council must confirm, modify or annul the decision by a qualified majority. If it fails to act within a deadline, the decision is abrogated.

These proposals for handling delegated legislation, known generically as comitology, aroused great concern among the other institutions. The Commission issued a declaration pointing out that under 3(b) and Safeguard (b), the Council had given itself the power to block implementing proposals even if it was unable to provide an alternative, thus frustrating the purpose of the primary legislation. The Commission announced that it would refrain from putting forward proposals under these two headings. The Parliament attempted to take the Council to the Court, but the latter ruled that Article 173 did not a constitute a legal base for the action. Subsequently the Parliament has attempted to replace all 3(a) and 3(b) proposals with 2(a) and 2(b) on the first reading of the primary legislation and block all 3(b) proposals on second reading, but this has not proved effective and comitology has given the Council a stranglehold on the content of implementing legislation; as a result these measures are increasingly a matter for negotiations between governments than for straightforward Commission proposals. It is a classic example of the way in which the Council appears to concede ground to the other institutions while actually clawing back power and consolidating its position as *primus inter pares*.[3]

The Council of Ministers is the most powerful of all the Brussels institutions; it is also the most secretive. Increasingly European Union legislation is the product of deals between national civil servants arrived at behind closed doors, so not even the ministers nominally responsible for taking the decisions understand how they were reached. Council press releases detail the content of decisions but give no clue as to who voted for what. Individual members frequently brief their national journalists, explaining how hard they fought the national corner and what remarkable concessions were achieved, but there is no way of checking; frequently the minister from a different member state is giving a wholly contradictory account in the next room. National parliaments, to whom ministers are theoretically accountable, have no say in the decision-making process; the results are so heavily negotiated that it is impossible to make subsequent changes without unravelling the entire agreement. In explaining decisions subsequently, ministers take refuge in the Council's institutional anonymity, and national parliamentarians have no means of knowing what their minister actually said or did.[4]

The opacity of the Council's decision-making is a major cause of lack of public confidence in the European Union. Commentators and politicians frequently rail at 'Brussels' for making allegedly daft decisions, oblivious to the fact that more often than not their own national officials have been party to the agreement, or even promoted it as part of some elaborate deal to protect the national interest. Unfortunately, human nature being what it is officials find it convenient to blame 'Brussels', by which they mean the Commission, for unpopular measures for which they themselves have been responsible. Among recent examples, which caused an outcry in the British press, were the notorious Meat Directives which sought to establish common standards of hygiene in abattoirs where the meat produced was intended for export. Because these directives were designed to regulate cross-border trade the legislation contained wide-ranging exemptions for locally traded meat, so much so that the Ministry of Agriculture could have exempted almost any abattoir it wished. Because there was a national policy, which quite properly was designed to remove large numbers of small traditional slaughterhouses, the exemptions were used very sparingly and large numbers were forced to close. Invariably this was blamed on Brussels meddling, whereas in fact the Ministry of Agriculture had not only endorsed the measures, but deliberately refused to make use of their powers to alleviate the effect.

Following the Maastricht negotiations an attempt was made to open Council proceedings to public scrutiny. This effort at transparency had the enthusiastic support of the British Prime Minister, John Major. Although there were some attempts to televise Council proceedings under the subsequent Danish Presidency, the media were quickly bored by lengthy and vacuous ministerial speeches; it was if the ministers had set out to prove that no one was interested in their proceedings. The experiment was discontinued and the Council of the European Union remains the only legislature in the western world whose proceedings are routinely closed to public scrutiny. The excuse is that national delegations would find it impossible to negotiate freely if their deliberations were open to the gaze of their national parliaments; public opinion would not tolerate explicit concessions of the national interest, so no decisions could be reached. This is simple sophistry: national parliaments have a right to know when these concessions are made and to hold their ministers to account. Council secrecy prevents this happening, with the result that there is no proper parliamentary scrutiny and the decisions of the European Union, which affect the lives of millions of citizens, frequently appear arbitrary and perverse. As long as democratic principle is subordinated to administrative convenience the processes of legislation will remain opaque and appear sinister. Lack of public confidence in the Brussels institutions and therefore the European Union is the direct result of ministerial secretiveness and an unwillingness on the part of national bureaucrats to allow the public to understand the manner of reaching decisions that are taken in their name.

The original treaties were framed on the basis that intergovernmental relationships were not sufficient to provide the degree of integration necessary to avoid conflict; states' rights had to be balanced by the collective interest. The ECSC was the most federalist of the treaties actually removing key industries from national control. Since then the balance has swung massively in the other direction so that the Council plays a role which is far greater than was ever foreseen when the Treaty of Rome was drafted. Unanimity is perfectly acceptable when the decision to be taken is one of principle involving the transfer of power; it is quite impracticable as a means of amending and adopting detailed legislative texts. The tacit abandonment of the veto enshrined in the Luxembourg Compromise and the move to more majority voting is a recognition of the need to adjust the Council's procedures to meet the needs of its altered responsibilities, the more extensive the Council's role the more necessary majority voting becomes.

Those who demand that the powers of the Council should be further strengthened at the expense of the Commission are arguing for a Community which would be even less capable of taking decisions unless there was a significant increase in the incidence of majority voting and a parallel relaxation of the rules for qualified majorities. This would become all the more necessary if the Community were to expand beyond the present 15 members. Majorities can be coercive, and it is open to question whether national interests are better protected by a Commission which seeks to produce initiatives as the result of a consensus subject to ratification by the Council, or by a majority vote in which sovereign countries are openly compelled to accept decisions to which they were opposed. This is of particular importance to Britain, a country which frequently finds itself in a minority and which has used the various blocking mechanisms with great skill to prevent the`passage of legislation to which she is opposed from being adopted. The Council is of course a federal institution and majority voting gives it the explicit power to override the wishes of individual member states; more power for the Council would tend to accentuate rather than diminish the federal aspects of the Community. The only way to guarantee the rights of individual states would be to restore the veto, but the experience of the years between 1973 and 1985 has shown this is a recipe for impotence; while the veto is indubitably a means of protecting member states from legislation they do not want, it is also a means of preventing them from securing their positive objectives. Presumably it was because she understood this that Margaret Thatcher signed up to the Single European Act.

These questions need to be addressed if the Community is to move forward. The development of the Council's role has moved the EC far away from the original conception and the mechanisms established by the Treaties have to be radically adjusted to reflect this. Much clearer thinking and openness of debate is required if this is to be achieved and the essential balance between the supranational and the national needs to be redefined and addressed. As things stand these issues are obscured from public debate by the continuing ambivalence of the governments which, while accepting the principle of collective action, find it difficult to admit that this necessarily involves a surrender of national sovereignty. The result is confusion about the nature of the Community and uncertainty as to its future; no wonder the ordinary citizen does not know what to make of it all.

4 The European Parliament: The democratic deficit

The Treaty of Paris, 1951, established a Common Assembly as one of the institutions of the Coal and Steel Community. With 78 delegates nominated by their respective national parliaments, it was required to meet at least once a year on the second Tuesday in March and could be convened for an extraordinary session at the request of the Council or the High Authority. It was further required to discuss the general report submitted by the High Authority and could put questions to it orally or in writing. Acting by a two-thirds majority of its members, it could dismiss the High Authority, though it had no say in the appointment of its successor. Article 21 (3) empowered the Assembly to draw up proposals for its own election by direct universal suffrage in accordance with a uniform procedure, this to be adopted unanimously by the Council and recommended to the member states.

The Treaty of Rome virtually reproduced the language of its predecessor and there was no significant change to the Assembly's functions though its numbers were increased to 142. However in numerous articles of the Treaty the Council was required to seek the opinion of the Assembly before acting on a Commission proposal, thus giving the deputies a modest role in the legislative process. A further 56 delegates, making 198 in all, were added when Britain, Denmark and Ireland joined the Community in 1973, though the Labour Party refused to take up its allocation of seats. From 1973 to the conclusion of the referendum in 1975 Britain was represented by 18 Conservatives who established themselves as a Group of European Conservatives with two Danish members, two Liberals and an independent peer.

The implementation of the Own Resources decision led to a substantial recasting of the Community's budgetary procedure which was adopted by Treaty amendment in 1970. This gave the Assembly an extra role as the Council's partner in adopting the Community budget. The revised Article 203 required the

Commission to prepare a Preliminary Draft Budget for submission to the Council before 1 September of the prior year. The Council then adopted an amended version of this as its draft budget within one month, and this was referred to the Assembly. The Assembly had 45 days to propose amendments to the Council's draft, acting by an absolute majority of its members. However when an item related to expenditure 'necessarily resulting from this Treaty or from acts adopted in accordance therewith' – so-called compulsory expenditure – the Assembly could only adopt modifications acting by a simple majority of votes cast. The Council required a qualified majority to alter or reject the Assembly's amendments; modifications required a qualified majority to sustain them, otherwise they were automatically rejected. Since 80 per cent of the expenditure in the budget was classified as compulsory, this was a major limitation on the Assembly's ability to alter the budget. The Council had 15 days to pronounce on the Assembly's proposed amendments and modifications after which the Assembly itself had 15 days to conduct a second reading; at this stage it had the power to amend or reject the Council's changes to its amendments by a majority of its members and three-fifths of the votes cast and could then proceed to adopt the budget. The President of the Assembly was required to declare the budget adopted and bring the procedure to its close. Alternatively under Article 203 (8) the Assembly, 'acting by a majority of its members and two thirds of the votes cast, may if there were important reasons, reject the draft budget and ask for a new draft to be submitted to it.'

Article 203 required the institutions to respect a maximum rate of increase in expenditure established by the Commission according to an abstruse set of econometric calculations. This could be increased by qualified majorities in the Council and Assembly acting together; as far as non-compulsory expenditure was concerned the Assembly had the right to adopt amendments up to half the maximum rate if the Council had increased expenditure by half the maximum rate across the budget as a whole. This so-called Parliamentary margin was the only area in which the Assembly had unfettered powers, but its area of application was minuscule.

However during the seventies the nominated Assembly developed its procedures for handling the budget and built up a substantial body of institutional expertise and experience. In particular it began to bargain with the Council over the use of its margin and sought to get concessions for its favoured projects. This provided a valuable legacy for its directly elected successor in 1979.

The main preoccupation of the Assembly was its drive for direct elections and its attempt to draw up the uniform electoral procedure foreseen by Article 138. The deputies sitting in Strasbourg were aware of the limitations of their mandate and their consequent weakness *vis à vis* the other institutions. Direct elections seemed the only way of establishing the European Parliament's democratic credentials. The national parliaments of the smaller member states, particularly the Dutch, were equally concerned to establish the Community as a democratic body, and worked closely with their nominated members to bring pressure on the member states. After much debate a uniform election procedure was drawn up but it was not adopted by the Council. Inevitably the system chosen was proportional, based on a system of regional lists. Such a solution was anathema to both the main parties in Britain who saw it as the thin end of the wedge, leading to proportional representation in national elections. The Callaghan Government introduced a bill to establish a proportional system for the European elections, but allowed a free vote. Predictably it was rejected and the ensuing European Council agreed that the election should be conducted in each country on the same procedures in force for national elections and incidentally that the new Euro MPs should be paid the same as their national counterparts. The only concession to uniformity was that although polling might take place on different days of the week, the declarations would be delayed until the last polling station had closed so the results would be synchronized. Thus in Britain although voting takes place on the traditional Thursday, we have to wait until the Sunday night for the count and result.

Polling duly took place on 14 June 1979 and the new Parliament convened on 17 July. There were now 410 members,[1] more than double the previous number, and the opening session was characterized by an immense sense of expectation. Although the 1979 election had not registered in Britain, which was still digesting the arrival of Mrs Thatcher in No. 10 Downing Street the previous month, on the Continent it had

captured the imagination. After the disappointments and set-
backs of the seventies it seemed that the Community had
acquired a new lease of life, and it had now come of age with
its democratic credentials established at last. The Founding
Fathers' dream of a united Europe seemed to have taken a
giant step forward and this was reflected in the speeches and
the massive press coverage of the inaugural session. Parliamentarians taking their seats for the first time were enthused by
feelings of high idealism and a sense that they were privileged
to be participating in the making of history. There were some
precedents, notably in the nineteenth-century German Diet,
but this was the first genuinely multinational, multilingual, directly elected parliament in history; for those present that July
day in Strasbourg seemed to herald the final defeat of nationalism and the dawning of a new age of harmony and peace.

The creation of a Parliament for Europe had been a long-
standing ambition for European federalists. They believed
that it was an essential building block in the construction of a
European system of government, providing it with an essential
democratic element. As power was transferred from the member states to the Community, the powers of national parliaments
were diminished as individual ministers could no longer be
held responsible for collective decisions adopted by a majority
vote; moreover since European law was superior to domestic
law, national parliaments had no authority in areas where the
Community was competent. This weakening of parliamentary
control, known as the democratic deficit, could only be made
good by increasing the power of the European Parliament so
the Council and Commission could be made democratically
accountable; the Parliament's relationship with them would
parallel that between national parliaments and national governments at Community level.

That at least was the theory; the reality was very different.
The original conception of the Assembly was deeply rooted in
French constitutional practice; Napoleon had direct experience
of the anarchy of the National Assembly and the Convention
during the French revolution and the system he bequeathed
kept the elected legislature firmly in its place. The role of
an assembly was to supervise the administration of the state
and confer legitimacy, it was not to interfere in the process of
government. Classically the role of a parliament is to install a

government, endorse its programme and approve the budget; it is the dignified part of the democratic system. This concept was reflected exactly in the powers conferred on the European Assembly – henceforward to be known as European Parliament – by the Treaties and although direct elections had vastly raised its profile they had added nothing to its competences. On one occasion British members had sought to exercise the power to dismiss the Commission, but with total lack of success. Subsequent attempts were to prove equally fruitless. It soon became clear that although Article 149 gave the Parliament a certain institutional status, it would never in foreseeable circumstances be used. Parliament could pass amendments to proposed legislation as part of its opinion, but there was no means of compelling the Council and Commission to consider them, let alone adopt them, so much of the procedure of examination in committee and adoption by the plenary session seemed little more than an empty charade. It was true that some scope for the exercise of Parliamentary power existed in the adoption of the budget, but the procedure was Byzantine in its complexity and certainly not designed to capture public imagination. Things were made worse by the fact that the dynamics of the budget meant that Parliament was invariably seeking more money to be allocated for Community spending, quickly earning itself the reputation of being hopelessly spendthrift, an image that was assiduously cultivated by the member states. Whereas most national parliaments had acquired their influence by defending the citizen against the exactions of the state, in the case of the European Parliament the reverse was true.

This institutional weakness was exacerbated by the circumstances surrounding the direct elections. The new members were a mixed bunch, no less than nine former prime ministers including Willy Brandt of West Germany and Michel Debré of France, took their places on 17 July, but the majority of members had no political experience whatever and several came from parties that had never expected to get elected. Of the 78 members from mainland Britain only 11 including two redoubtable ladies, Mrs Barbara Castle, Leader of the 18 strong British Labour Group, and Mrs Winifred Ewing, the lone Scots Nationalist, had previous parliamentary experience.[2] Moreover as the newly elected President, Mme Simone Veil, the former French Health Minister, was quickly to discover, the rules of procedure that had been appropriate for a nominated Assembly of 198 part-time members, were wholly inappropriate for the new 410-member full-time Parliament. The excessive protection the rules afforded for the individual member and the small political groups provided a rich vein of opportunity for mavericks such as the Italian radicals, Marco Panella and Emma Bonino,[3] who used them to disrupt proceedings in a manner that made the Parliament look badly organized and ridiculous. The image of the slightly dotty left still lingers 15 years later.

The atmosphere of chaos was exacerbated by the extraordinary working arrangements which compelled the Parliament to commute endlessly between Strasbourg, Luxembourg and Brussels. In 1957 the City of Luxembourg had been proposed as the site of all the Community institutions, making it in effect the capital of Europe. The City authorities turned them down because they feared their small provincial capital would be swamped by an influx of Eurocrats. As a result the Commission and Council were temporarily housed in Brussels while the Assembly met in Strasbourg. These arrangements were formalized as part of the 1965 Treaty which merged the institutions of the EC, ECSC and Euratom; the Commission and Council were based in Brussels, but had a fixed number of meetings each year in Luxembourg. The Parliament had its plenary sessions alternately in the Council of Europe's building in Strasbourg and a custom-built chamber in Luxembourg where its administration was based, but its Committees met in Brussels so as to accommodate the Commission. Facilities in all three centres were wholly inadequate and a rash of public building commenced which added to the Parliament's reputation for extravagance and waste. The plenary sessions in Luxembourg were quite soon dropped with the result that the brand-new debating chamber has hardly ever been used. Strasbourg with the enthusiastic backing of successive French governments fought tenaciously to obtain the seat of the Parliament on a permanent basis; a substantial group of parliamentarians, led by the British Conservatives Alan Tyrrell and Peter Price, was equally determined to locate the Parliament on a single site in Brussels, and a kind of guerrilla warfare involving procedural coups and counter coups and actions before the Court of Justice has been taking place ever since. To the dismay of the Brussels faction the 1992 Edinburgh Summit moved to formalize the status quo by declaring Strasbourg was the seat of the European Parliament and 12 sessions had to be held there each year including the budget session. It would take a determined effort by a large majority of the Parliament to change this. As things now stand Strasbourg continues to stage the plenary sessions and is building a new hemicycle to accommodate the enlarged Parliament; Brussels has a new, large hemicycle where so-called mini-sessions are held most months in tandem with committee meetings, and the rump of the Administration remains at Luxembourg. Members remain divided in their affections between Brussels and Strasbourg and it is still not clear which has the upper hand. The image of an itinerant Parliament accompanied by its paperwork contained in a wagon train of metal containers shuttling endlessly between three centres has done nothing to enhance its public reputation.

The inexperience of the majority of the newly elected members meant that those who had survived from the nominated Assembly naturally became the leaders of the new parliamentary groups and were supported by an administration which was rooted in the ways of the past. As a result the institutional habits of the nominated Assembly continued long after direct elections, with disastrous results for the Parliament's understanding of its role. The nominated members, fixated by the original treaties, had seen themselves primarily as working with the Commission to advance the interests of the Community, and in a state of permanent negotiation with the Council to extend their own power and influence in small increments. Although lofty sentiments about representing the citizens of Europe were frequently expressed in the Hemicycle, few members had any meaningful contacts with their domestic electorates and there were almost none at all with national parliaments, with whom relations were normally characterized by mutual suspicion and disdain. Instead of striking out boldly to establish itself as a popular assembly, representing the interests of people against those of the establishment in the shape of the Council and Commission, the directly elected Parliament quickly became a co-conspirator in an interinstitutional game whereby the competences of the Community were to be steadily pushed forward irrespective of popular consent.

In short, for all the razzmatazz and genuine idealism that characterized the first directly elected Parliament, it laboured under very severe handicaps. Its competences fell far short of its pretensions. Its membership was disparate, elected under different systems with widely differing views of what the MEP's role should be, politically inexperienced and naive. Its rules of procedure and working conditions were inadequate and made it look absurd and its leadership, rooted firmly in the ways of the nominated Assembly, was to prove incapable of rising to the challenge of establishing its popular legitimacy. It is remarkable that the European Parliament in spite of these handicaps has successfully increased its powers and actually enhanced its influence *vis à vis* the Commission and Council.

The first serious business to be addressed by the new directly elected Parliament was the 1980 budget procedure, indeed the Commissioner responsible for the budget, Christopher Tugendhat of the United Kingdom, presented his preliminary draft budget to the inaugural session. The background was a considerable crisis in the Community's finances. Thanks to the Common Agricultural Policy (CAP), farm production had raced ahead of demand in the seventies and the resulting surpluses were required to be bought up and stored by the Commission, before being disposed of in third country markets as heavily subsidized exports. Distress sales of cut price butter and other commodities to Russia were extremely unpopular and disrupted international markets, but the cost of storage of ever increasing quantities of cereals and dairy products was prohibitive. By 1979 over 70 per cent of the budget was being absorbed by expenditure on the CAP, leaving no room at all for the Parliament's preferred priorities for spending, such as regional and social policy and overseas aid. Attempts to reorder priorities ran into opposition in the Council from the French, Irish, Danish and other governments determined to maintain payments to their farmers, which from their point of view was what made the Community worth while. The Council of Budget Ministers, conscious of the need to restrain their domestic deficits, made substantial cuts in the Commission's proposals for increases in non-compulsory expenditure, while preserving intact compulsory expenditure over which it had unfettered control. Prompted by its Budget Rapporteur, the Dutch Socialist Piet Dankert, the Parliament restored the cuts with interest at its first reading thanks to an extremely liberal interpretation of its margin. The Council, not accustomed to such parliamentary bravura, reacted badly and threw out all the Parliament's amendments; Dankert and the Budget Committee were determined to stand firm and on 12 December the Parliament rejected the budget for 'the good and important reaons' that it was inadequate for the Community to carry out the tasks facing it. There was an atmosphere of near-revolutionary excitement in the Hemicycle and the President in Office of the Budget Council, the Irishman Brian Lenihan, himself a former MEP, was moved to describe the newly elected Parliament as an undisciplined, disorderly rabble.

Following rejection of the budget, Article 204 of the Treaty applies and spending is restricted to a maximum of one-twelfth of the previous year's expenditure until such time as a new budget is adopted. This can be increased if both halves of the Budgetary Authority, that is Council and Parliament, agree. In 1980 agreement was finally reached in June on a budget involving some modest concessions to the Parliament on the use of its margin, but the initial rejection of the budget inaugurated an era of institutional squabbling which lasted until 1987. The dispute with the Council over the budget became an annual saga, with Parliament and the Commission trying to break the Council insistence on keeping non-compulsory expenditure in check so as to maintain the level of spending on agriculture without breaching the budgetary ceiling. Matters were hugely complicated by the parallel row over the British budget rebate; the Parliament objected strongly to the concept of *juste retour*, the idea that there should be a broad balance between contributions and receipts encapsulated in Mrs Thatcher's famous demand, 'I want my money back.' The temporary settlement of 1982 gave the Budget Committee some extra leverage as it was required to endorse the British rebate as part of the budgetary package; it was able to hold the rebate hostage in an attempt to blackmail the Council into making concessions on spending levels and met with some modest success, to the fury of the British Government which rightly suspected that the Parliament was determined to deny its rebate. Meanwhile the Community's finances became increasingly chaotic and stretched; all kinds of procedural devices were used by the Commission to maintain essential payments.

Finally in 1987 at Fontainebleau the European Council agreed to raise the budgetary ceiling in return for a five-year interinstitutional agreement which divided expenditure into five categories and established a annual ceiling for each. In return for lifting her veto on increasing Own Resources, Britain's rebate was put on a permanent footing and considerably more money was made available for the Structural Funds[4] to make room for the accession of Spain and Portugal. A similar agreement which took account of the effects of the Maastricht Treaty and covering the years from 1993–7 was concluded at the Edinburgh Summit in December 1992; it was ratified finally after a close vote in the House of Commons at the end of 1994, eight Conservative rebels losing the Party Whip in the process.

The annual budgetary procedure was the main focus of attention for the directly elected Parliament. It represented the one area where real power had been inherited from its predecessor and the Parliamentary leadership saw it as the obvious field for an extension of its influence. Considerable drama attended the meetings of the Budget Committee with the President of the Budget Council regularly summoned to late night meetings to account for his failings. The Committee itself acquired considerable prestige and its leading figures such as Piet Dankert, the German Horst Langes and Britain's David Curry acquired a considerable mastery of the abstruse procedures, playing their hand with verve and skill. Concessions were wrung from the Council and the Parliament as a whole increased its weight within the institutional triangle. However by accepting the interinstitutional agreement of 1987 the Budget Committee effectively surrendered its capacity for initiative in return for stability and the recognition of its right to reallocate expenditure within some categories. The budget procedure is now automatic and the drama that characterized the early eighties has disappeared. In its place is the renegotiation of the interinstitutional agreement every five years but even this now takes place within strictly defined limits.

Unfortunately the debates on the budget did nothing to improve the Parliament's standing among the electorate. Since it had no responsibility for raising taxes, only for spending the money, it was all too easy for the Council to depict it as spendthrift, only interested in increasing its own power at the taxpayers' expense. In Britain opposition to the rebate gave it a very bad press and the sense of chaos and drift surrounding the Community's finances did nothing to enhance its overall reputation. Its failure to use the power of discharge to attack maladministration and fraud and its easy acceptance of the Commission's demands completed an unhappy picture. In the end the European Parliament failed to establish a dominant position over the Budget because its aims were not understood and it had therefore no popular support for what it was trying to achieve.

Outside the Budget Committee the dominant figure of the first Parliament was the Italian Altiero Spinelli, who had briefly been a Commissioner in the 1970s. Spinelli had been imprisoned on the island of Ventotene for 16 years during Mussolini's dictatorship and during that time had become a committed federalist. After the war he became one of the leading campaigners for a united Europe, but was constantly frustrated by the failure of the European Community to match the grandeur of his vision. Following the elections Spinelli and a number of his supporters founded the Crocodile Club, named after one of Strasbourg's finest restaurants, to work for rapid progress in the establishment of a Federal European State. In 1981 the so-called Crocodile Resolution was adopted by an enthusiastic Parliament; the resolution called for a special committee to be set up with the task of drafting a new Treaty of Union to replace the Treaty of Rome; it would be adopted by the European Parliament and presented to the national parliaments for enactment following the next direct elections, which would serve as a popular endorsement.

The Institutional Committee was established and with the assistance of some expert constitutional lawyers the draft Treaty was duly drawn up. It was adopted by the Parliament in March 1984 and set out a blueprint for a federal state, with the European Parliament representing the people enjoying equality of power with the Council representing the states. The Union would assume all the basic powers of a state including the right to levy taxes and to declare war and peace. Spinelli's draft treaty remains the most complete exposition of the shape and nature of a United States of Europe; he was a romantic who believed passionately that popular opinion would readily endorse his concept of a federal union as the natural expression of a united Europe, if only it could be put to them without

being distorted by national governments with vested interests to protect. He failed to appreciate the extent to which the
concept of the nation-state is entrenched in the popular consciousness so that the natural focus of individual patriotism is
the country rather than the Continent. The draft Treaty hardly
figured in the 1984 election campaign and although it received
some support from the Italian and Belgian Parliaments, the
others ignored it as simply eccentric. Although it was quickly
put aside, the Spinelli Draft Treaty remains the ultimate federalist aspiration of the European Parliament and has been
the foundation of its submissions to the two subsequent intergovernmental conferences. The Single European Act was to
some extent inspired by the draft Treaty, though Spinelli himself regarded it as hopelessly inadequate.

Less dramatic, but in the long term more effective, was the
progress made in establishing the Parliament's legislative role.
Just before direct elections in 1979 the Court of Justice gave
an important judgment in which it ruled that where the Treaty
required the Council to receive an opinion from the European
Parliament, it could not act until the resolution containing that
opinion had been duly adopted and transmitted.[5] There was
no obligation on the Council to do more than take note of the
opinion, but it could not complete the legislative process without it. About the same time a statement by its President, Roy
Jenkins, confirmed that the Commission was bound by formal
statements made on its behalf to Parliament.

Building on the Isoglucose Case and the Commission President's declaration, Parliament's constitutional experts, led by
the British MEP Christopher Prout, drafted new rules of procedure designed to give Parliament the ability to delay legislation if its amendments were ignored. Before the final vote on
a legislative resolution, the Rapporteur could ask the Commission whether they were prepared to accept Parliament's amendments and incorporate them in their proposal. The answer
would be binding on the Commission. If the answer was unsat-
isfactory the Rapporteur could request the resolution to be sent
back to committee for further consideration so that further
negotiations could take place; as long as the resolution containing Parliament's opinion was not passed the proposal was
effectively blocked.

This innovative change to the rules of procedure, reflecting

British constitutional practice which is based on precedent rather than legislation, had the potential to enhance Parliament's ability to make its amendments stick. In fact it was rarely used. The procedural niceties did not appeal to parliamentarians, who much preferred the visionary grandeur of the Spinelli approach, while the habit of co-operation with the Commission had become so entrenched that there was an instinctive reluctance to hold up a Commission proposal or reject their advice on amendments. For all that, the approach adopted by Prout and his collaborators became the basis of the Cooperation Procedure established by the Single European Act, and proved a most effective means of extending the Parliament's powers.

Following the establishment of the Customs Union, so-called non-tariff barriers to trade, frequently in the form of unique national standards, were routinely used by member states to protect domestic producers from external competition. With the exception of agricultural products, the Common Market described in the Treaty was little more than a myth. In 1980 a British Conservative, Basil de Ferranti, and two Germans, the Christian Democrat Karl von Wogau, and Socialist Dieter Rogalla who was a former Commission official, founded the Kangaroo Group for parliamentarians committed to the removal of barriers to trade and the abolition of border controls.[6] The Kangaroos developed into an effective pressure group and their Tuesday lunches in Strasbourg became a regular platform for campaigners against the retention of customs posts at the internal frontiers of the Community.

Rather more cerebral was an initiative by Sir Fred Catherwood, MEP for Cambridgeshire and a former director general of NEDEC and latterly of the Overseas Trade Board. He persuaded Piet Dankert, who succeeded Simone Veil as President of the Parliament in 1982, to commission a study of the causes of Euro-sclerosis by Michel Albert, a former Commissaire Général du Plan, and Professor James Ball of the London Business School. The Albert-Ball Report on European Economic Recovery set out to quantify the costs to industry of the fragmented internal market, the 'Cost of Non-Europe' as they termed it. Prompted by Sir Fred Catherwood, Dankert set up an ad hoc Committee on European Economic Recovery which held a series of hearings on the conclusions of Albert and

Ball; their report, drafted by a Belgian rapporteur, Fernand Herman, recommended the removal of all barriers to trade and the establishment of freedom of movement of goods and services within a single integrated economic space. The Herman report, adopted by the Parliament just before the elections of 1984, provided the basic inspiration for the Single Market Programme launched by the incoming Commission President, Jacques Delors, in 1985.[7]

The achievements of the first directly elected Parliament are not to be despised. By its rejection of the 1980 budget and the subsequent battles over Community funding it established itself as a significant institutional partner of the Commission and Council, even though it never achieved its ambition of becoming the key player in the budgetary process. The development of the consultation procedure flowing from its use of the Isoglucose case strengthened its legislative role and the work of the Kangaroo Group and the Albert-Ball Report laid the foundations for the Single Market. The Spinelli Treaty, though it never achieved public acceptance, provided the element of vision and inspiration that the Community of the seventies so obviously lacked. Given the immense handicaps with which it started, the first directly elected Parliament can fairly claim some notable successes. Its overriding failure was in not establishing itself in the popular imagination as a genuine defender of citizens rights or establishing any kind of democratic accountability over the Council and Commission. The gravamen of the charge against a Parliament of radicals is that it failed to be radical enough and was prepared to settle for recognition from the establishment rather than campaign for the support of the people as Spinelli had wished.

The second directly elected Parliament, 1984–9, was generally less distinguished than its predecessor and more predictable. The French returned eight far-right deputies from the Front National, led by Jean-Marie le Pen, who immediately became universal hate figures, ostracized by the other groups. In return they did their best to disrupt proceedings by insisting on numerous time-consuming roll-call votes and baited the Socialists with their anti-immigrant, nationalist posturing. On the other side of the spectrum a Green Group of 18 members appeared for the first time; they acted as a pole of attraction for left-wing members of the Socialist Group, so both the big groups were under pressure from their extreme wings. The influence of the Greens was particularly marked in their use of the urgency procedure;[8] every Thursday a string of resolutions calling attention to alleged human rights violations were forced on to the agenda. Many were poorly researched, based on unsubstantiated press reports and hearsay and frequently caused grave offence to the governments to whom they were addressed. The Americans were particular sufferers, regularly castigated as international oppressors, and the Turks also came in for much criticism. This kind of self-indulgent posturing did nothing to help the Parliament's international reputation. The leaders of the two largest political groups, Rudi Arndt of the Socialists and Egon Klepsch of the Christian Democrats, both Germans, reacted to these centrifugal tendencies by co-operating closely together especially in making sure that Parliament was able to deliver the required qualified majorities after the Single European Act came into force. As a result the two big groups were able to control the main agenda while the fringe groups struck attitudes.

The second five-year mandate was dominated by the launch of the 1992 Single Market Programme and the Single European Act (SEA). Parliament enthusiastically embraced the former, for which it could reasonably claim some credit and proved an effective partner in getting the 300 directives proposed in the Cockfield White Paper through the legislative system. Much to the disappointment of the Institutional Committee, it was not represented on the Dooge Committee which prepared the ground for the 1986 Intergovernmental Conference and the Spinelli draft Treaty was ignored by the member states. However although the Treaty amendments incorporated in the SEA fell well short of Parliament's ambitions, some procedural innovations were introduced which significantly extended its legislative competence.

Article 149 established the Co-operation Procedure which meant that Parliamentary amendments to single market legislation had to be taken much more seriously by the Council. Where the Treaty stipulated that this procedure should be used the Council would consult the Parliament on a Commission proposal in the usual way. The Council, after considering any amendments, would adopt a common position, in effect its own version of the proposal. The Parliament then had three months to propose further amendments or reject the common position, in each case by an absolute majority of its members, or 260 votes. In the event of a rejection the Council had to be unanimous to adopt the common position. The Commission then had one month to consider amendments proposed by the Parliament on second reading. Those it accepted became part of its own proposal and could be adopted by a qualified majority in the Council, but unanimity was required to adopt amendments which the Commission did not support.

There were plenty of pitfalls in this elaborate procedure and there were doubts as to whether Parliament would have sufficient self discipline to operate it effectively. In the event the Rules Committee, prompted by its rapporteur Christopher Prout, and supported by the Arndt-Klepsch axis, produced a set of amendments to the Rules of Procedure which enabled the Parliament to implement the Cooperation Procedure with considerable dispatch and economy of effort, building on the precedents established following the Isoglucose Case.

In practice the Co-operation Procedure did not produce the results that the Parliament's supporters had expected. Parliamentarians proved extremely reluctant to reject proposals; they felt they were elected to pass legislation, not defeat it. Similarly the Council stuck together in the face of Parliament's new partnership with the Commission, member states were most reluctant to break ranks and so the necessary unanimity could always be found to defeat unwelcome amendments whatever the individual positions might have been. As a result there are very few examples of major changes being forced through but the Commission and Council did find it expedient to accept substantial numbers of amendments at first reading and even some at second reading, so the Parliament's role as an advisory and amending chamber was very much enhanced. This was particularly true of SEA legislation, the Committee for Economic and Monetary Affairs and Industrial Policy (EMAC) proved most diligent in examining proposals in detail and produced a number of minor but appropriate amendments. Lobbyists were quick to appreciate the Parliament's potential for improving proposals and it attracted a great deal of specialized attention as a result. Increasingly trade associations and other representative organizations saw it as a useful forum in which their concerns could be expressed.

A further innovation in the SEA, scarcely noticed at the time but with substantial implications for the future, was the Assent Procedure introduced in Article 237 which covered applications from states wishing to join the Community, and Article 238 dealing with association agreements establishing special trading relations with third countries. In both cases the European Parliament was required to assent to the agreement by an absolute majority, that is 260 votes were required in favour of an accession treaty or an association agreement for it to become effective. It seems likely that the negotiators at the IGC failed to appreciate the potential of the Assent Procedure, but Parliament itself was quick to exploit it. Renewal of the Association Agreement with Israel was blocked until she made concessions to Palestinian vegetable and fruit producers by allowing them direct access to European markets, and the Association Agreement with Syria was frozen following criticism of her human rights record. One may query the advisability of mixing trade and political issues in this way, but the Parliament showed considerable dexterity in exploiting its opportunity and established itself as an influence to be reckoned with in these third country relationships. There were already suggestions that Article 237 would prove a useful weapon when the next group of accession agreements came up for consideration; there would be a price to be paid in institutional terms if Parliament's assent was to be forthcoming.

By the third direct elections in 1989, the Parliament had made significant gains in the institutional trialogue and was accepted as a partner, albeit a tiresome one, by the Council and Commission. It certainly could not be ignored. It had demonstrated that it was capable of acting quickly and effectively when the need arose, and its revised rules of procedure had provided some much needed discipline. The increased concentration of staff at Brussels had improved efficiency and encouraged a greater sense of professionalism, which was recognized by those whose business brought them regularly into contact with its members. On the debit side the Parliament had again failed to achieve any kind of popular recognition; its electorate remained largely ignorant of its activities and certainly did not see it as defending their interests. Indeed those aspects which did occasionally surface in the public consciousness tended to confirm the image of impotence, extravagance and dottiness. No forceful personalities had emerged as Parliamentary leaders and few ambitious politicians looked to Strasbourg for their careers. Most worrying of all the Parliament was almost the last redoubt of the federalist vision and as such increasingly out of touch with the people on whose behalf it claimed to speak.

Part of the problem lay in the arcane procedures by which the Community transacted its business; lack of transparency and the absence of public interest encouraged Parliamentarians to ride their personal hobby horses to a point where the institution became more a forum for special interests than the authentic voice of the people of Europe. Although now and again it did rise to the occasion and give expression to the sentiments of the majority of Europeans on major issues of the day, these were exceptions, not the rule.[9] For the most part Parliamentarians pursued their special interests with varying degrees of diligence, enjoying the status of elected representatives, but doing little that seemed relevant to their electors. European elections were not taken seriously, so many were elected who would never have been considered as candidates for national office. In Strasbourg and Brussels members were effectively insulated from the pressure of opinion at home, free to indulge their prejudices, confident that somehow or other they were contributing to a better world but never taken seriously as politicians. This being the case there was no incentive to behave responsibly, so apart from the budget there was little attempt to use the powers that existed in a constructive way; the second directly elected Parliament spent most of its time making ineffectual gestures and sounded increasingly querulous in its demand for more powers.

The Parliament has never established its democratic legitimacy in the eyes of the people it purports to represent and that remains its greatest weakness. This was highlighted in the most shameful manner in the aftermath of Maastricht when the Parliament totally failed to give expression to the widespread popular doubts surrounding the Treaty. Apart from the French National Front and some elements on the extreme left, the European Parliament failed to challenge any of the assumptions of Maastricht, indeed it championed the cause of faster integration at a time when the tide of public opinion was flowing rapidly in the other direction; it was left to the Danish electorate to blow the whistle with its 'No' vote in June 1992. The European Parliament, which should have been the forum for the expression of public anxiety, was so obsessed with advancing its powers within the institutional framework, that it failed to notice what was happening in the world outside.

5 The European Court of Justice: Legislation by judges?*

The role of the European Court of Justice (ECJ), is described in Article 164 of the Treaty of Rome in somewhat Delphic terms:

> The Court of Justice shall ensure that in the interpretation and application of this Treaty the law is observed.

The concept of freedom under the law which is enshrined in the American Constitution is central to modern democratic theory, the fundamental insight being that free societies can only exist if there is a set of rules, common to all and impartially applied, which regulate the mutual obligations and rights of individuals and are based on a general consensus. The alternative to the rule of law is anarchy or everyone for himself. The need for a legal framework is just as important for groups of nations as it is for groups of individuals.

In the United States, Congress has the right to propose amendments to the Constitution which must then be approved by a majority of states; the Supreme Court has the task of interpreting the Constitution and applying its principles in circumstances that could not possibly have been foreseen when the Constitution was drafted. This is in contrast to the situation in Britain, where there is no written constitution; the Queen in Parliament is the supreme constitutional authority and the courts are required to interpret the law as passed by Parliament and have a duty to ensure that it is universally applied. Judicial review enables the courts to hear complaints that Ministers, who are responsible to Parliament, have not complied with the law and can issue declarations which remain effective until the law is changed. In France the Conseil d'Etat is the final arbiter of constitutional questions, while in Germany the Federal Constitutional Court at Karlsruhe is

---

* A bibliography follows this chapter. See p. 74.

responsible for ensuring that the Federal Constitution is respected; it was this court which had to decide whether the Maastricht Treaty was compatible with the Constitution and so capable of being ratified by the Bundestag.

In a federal system the constitutional court has the additional duty of ruling on the division of powers between the federal government and the states. In such systems the court is an equal constitutional partner of the legislature with its own autonomous status; it can declare acts of the legislature unconstitutional. This could not happen in a unitary state such as Britain where the courts are quite clearly subordinate to the legislature. The European Union is a quasi-federation with a written constitution in the shape of the Treaties. It therefore follows that the Court of Justice should play a role similar to that of a federal constitutional court, and be responsible for ensuring that the balance between the supranational institutions and the states is maintained and the institutions exercise their powers in the manner prescribed by the treaties. Since the Court itself is autonomous and established by treaty its jurisprudence was always likely to be biased towards the realization of the Treaty's central aim of 'Ever Closer Union' and so it has proved.

The ECJ has 15 judges, one from each of the member states. The judges are assisted by seven advocates-general, officials who have no counterpart in the British legal system. They have the status and precedence of judges and are required to prepare a preliminary opinion for the guidance of the Court following the hearing and submissions, but before the Court begins its deliberations. In some ways, as Wyatt and Dashwood point out, the advocate-general's opinion can be considered as a preliminary judgment to guide the Court proper, so that there are two judicial considerations of the case without resorting to an appeal procedure. In practice the Court usually, but not invariably, follows the advocate-general's opinion, which is published alongside the judgment and may be cited as a precedent in subsequent cases.

Article 167 lays down that the judges and advocates-general must be chosen by common accord of the member states,

> from persons whose independence is beyond doubt and who possess the qualifications required for appointment to the highest judicial offices in their respective countries or who are jurisconsults of recognised competence.

There is no requirement that the member states be equally represented, but in practice one judge per country plus one has always been the rule.

The Court operates for the most part by written procedure, though there is normally an oral hearing at which the judges can put direct questions to the parties. Deliberation is in secret and the opinion is written by a judge rapporteur who is appointed by the President of the Court. All judgments are presented as the judgment of the Court as a whole; there is no provision for dissenting opinions and this adds to the significance of the advocate-general's role. The Court is normally divided into chambers of three or five judges; member states or the institutions can request that a case be heard by the full Court in plenary session.

The Single European Act (SEA) contained a provision enabling the Council, following a request by the ECJ, to establish a Court of First Instance to hear 'certain classes of action or proceeding brought by natural or legal persons', but not member states or institutions, with a possibility of appeal to the ECJ. The Court of First Instance (CFI) was duly established in 1989 and shares premises with the ECJ in Luxembourg. The Court, which has 12 judges, hears cases on disputes between the EC and its servants, certain actions brought against the Commission under Articles 33 and 35 of the ECSC Treaty,[1] and actions brought in connection with competition policy. Although the ECJ suggested that it should also hear cases on anti-dumping and the Common Commercial Policy, this was rejected by the Council, prompted by France. The main purpose of the CFI was to relieve the case load of the ECJ itself and speed up decision-making and also to develop a core of judicial expertise in specialized areas such as competition policy and the staff regulations. It is too early to say how successful this experiment has been, but it is possible to envisage that, as the Union expands, a more elaborate system will become necessary with separate Courts dealing with specific areas of policy and the ECJ itself acting as the Constitutional Court and Court of Appeal. Indeed it has been suggested that courts of this type take over some of the quasi-judicial functions of the Commission itself.

The European Community exists in consequence of an international agreement between sovereign states, but the jurisdiction of the ECJ is quite different to other international tribunals such as the International Court of Justice which sits in The Hague. These courts hear suits between states that are parties to international treaties and conventions which create specific rights and obligations; they make judgments on the substance of the Treaties. Such judgments are declaratory, with no direct effect in the countries concerned, and the Court has no power of enforcement. Although Article 170 of the Treaty of Rome gives a member state which considers that one of its partners has failed to fulfil an obligation under the Treaty the right to bring the matter before the ECJ following a reasoned opinion from the Commission, this possibility has only been used on one occasion when France brought an action against the UK.[2] Interestingly the United Kingdom resisted the temptation to retaliate three years later, when it declined to bring an action against France for its refusal to permit the import of UK-produced lamb, but instead called on the Commission to take action under Article 169 and enforce the rules against the French. It seems that the member states prefer to leave the Commission to act as guardian of the Treaties, rather than disturb the unity of the Council by initiating actions themselves. Although customary international law contributes to the jurisprudence of the ECJ, it has not developed this aspect very far.

Other international courts are established by the states parties to a Treaty or Convention with the express purpose of adjudicating disputes over the way in which they carry out their obligations. An obvious example is the European Court of Human Rights which sits in Strasbourg and is frequently confused with the ECJ. This court hears cases referred to it by the Commission of Human Rights when a signatory has failed to carry out its obligations to its citizens and has not provided them with a remedy in domestic law. Such cases are confined to alleged breaches of the Convention and the court judgments cannot create new individual rights and obligations which are not enshrined therein.

The ECJ has some of the characteristics of a federal constitutional court and the nature of its role gives the European Union a unique character. The underlying principles of its jurisprudence are set out in *Costa* v. *ENEL* in 1964:[3]

By creating a Community of unlimited duration, having its own institutions, its own personality, its own legal capacity of representation on the international plane, and more particularly, real powers stemming from the limitation of sovereignty or a transfer of powers from the states to the Community, the Member States have limited their sovereign rights, albeit within limited fields, and have created a body of law which binds both their individuals and themselves.

This independent and overarching legal system is founded on the three pillars of direct applicability, direct effect and primacy.

The five types of Community instrument – regulations, directives, decisions, recommendations and opinions – are described in Article 189 of the Treaty of Rome. The last two have no binding effect, but the others create laws which are binding on the member states to whom they are addressed and must be enforced by the national courts:

> A regulation shall have general application. It shall be binding in its entirety and directly applicable in all Member States.
> A directive shall be binding as to the result to be achieved, upon each Member State to which it is addressed, but shall leave to the national authorities the choice of form and methods.
> A decision shall be binding in its entirety upon those to whom it is addressed.

Direct effect takes direct application one step further by providing that national courts must give effect to rights and obligations accruing to individuals as a consequence of directly applicable Community law. The basic case is *van Gend and Loos*[4] in which the ECJ was asked to rule whether the Treaty could be invoked by one of its own nationals against a member state which had introduced new customs regulations contrary to Article 12.[5] The judgment states:

> Independently of the legislation of Member States, Community law therefore not only imposes obligations on individuals but is also intended to confer upon them rights which become part of their legal heritage. These rights arise not only where they are expressly granted by the Treaty, but also by reason of the obligations which the Treaty imposes in a clearly defined way upon individuals as well as upon Member States and upon the institutions of the Community.

The decision in *van Gend and Loos*, which has been extended and developed by subsequent judgments, places on national courts a duty to enforce Community law even when it is in apparent conflict with national legislation.

There is no specific reference in the Treaty to the primacy of Community over national law, though as far as the United Kingdom is concerned Section 2 (1) of the 1972 European Communities Act states explicitly that Community law shall taken precedence over national law where there is a conflict between the two. The general principle was stated by the ECJ in the Simmenthal case:[6]

> Every national court must, in a case within its jurisdiction apply Community law in its entirety and protect rights which the latter confers on individuals and must accordingly set aside any provision of national law which may conflict with it, whether prior or subsequent to the Community rule.

These judgments, which have been developed and extended in other cases, make it clear that there is a autonomous body of Community law, rooted in the Treaties, which must be applied directly by national courts irrespective of their domestic legislation, and which creates enforceable rights and obligations for Community citizens applying equally across the European Union. This body of law is essentially federal in character and has provided one of the main motors for the process of integration. The potential role of national courts in applying Community law is often not appreciated: they could and should be a dynamic element in the development of the legal system without constant recourse to the ECJ itself.

It is not surprising that the ECJ has been so heavily criticized in Britain. Not only does it represent a constitutional phenomenon with which the British are unfamiliar and ill at ease, but it also poses a direct challenge to the sovereignty of our own Parliament. The most painful example of this was the Factortame case in 1989.[7] As a result of the Common Fisheries Policy (CFP), quotas governing the amount of fish permitted to be caught were assigned to the member states to be divided among the national fishing fleet. The object was to conserve stocks by limiting catches and to achieve an equitable share out of a scarce resource. A number of Spanish fishing companies incorporated themselves in the United Kingdom and applied for a share of UK fishing quota. This would enable Spanish-owned vessels flying the British flag to fish in UK waters and land the catch directly in Spanish ports. Following complaints by West Country fishermen that UK quota was being diverted to the Spanish fishing fleet, the British Parliament enacted the 1988 Merchant Shipping Act which required ownership of companies applying for UK fishing quota to be in the hands of British nationals. The Spanish trawler owners sued the Secretary of State for Transport in the British courts. Following an appeal, the House of Lords referred the issue to the ECJ for an opinion and it confirmed that the Merchant Shipping Act was incompatible with European law as it discriminated against Community citizens on grounds of nationality, contrary to Articles 53 and 54(c) of the Treaty which guarantee freedom of establishment. In its subsequent judgment,[8] the House of Lords held that the effect of Section 2 (1) of the 1972 European Communities Act had the effect of adding a notional clause to the Merchant Shipping Act which stated that the Act was without prejudice to the directly enforceable rights of nationals of any member state of the EC. The British courts would therefore grant a judicial review to anyone claiming that his rights under European Community law were infringed by an Act of Parliament, a truly momentous change in British constitutional practice in that the courts could for the first time overturn an Act of Parliament. The Merchant Shipping Act was duly amended to remove the offending clauses.

The decision in *Factortame* should have come as no surprise, but it created considerable shock-waves by bringing home to public opinion the extent to which national sovereignty had been diminished by Community membership. As long as Britain remains subject to European law, it is not possible for Parliament to protect the economic interests of its own nationals. Although ultimate sovereignty remains at Westminster in so far as Parliament can always repeal the 1972 European Communities Act and render European law inoperative, the sense of impotence engendered by this decision was a powerful reinforcement for the arguments of the Eurosceptics in the House of Commons. Since then there have been numerous demands that the offending section of the 1972 Act should be repealed and the supremacy of the national courts restored. If this were to happen Britain could no longer continue as a member of the European Union in its present form.

Article 169 of the Treaty establishes the procedure whereby the Commission can bring a member state before the ECJ if it considers that it has failed to fulfil an obligation under the Treaty. Any legal person can complain to the Commission that a particular Article in the Treaty or Act of the Community has not been correctly implemented by a member state; the Commission is bound to investigate the complaint though it has complete discretion as to whether it will pursue the matter. If it does decide to do so the first stage in the process is an informal approach to the member state authorities asking for an explanation. This may be followed by a more formal exchange of letters and then the opening of an infringement procedure, a notice of which is published in the *Official Journal*; at this stage other interested parties are invited to make observations. Having received the member state's formal response and considered any observations, the Commission may decide to issue a reasoned opinion in which it sets out the facts giving rise to the complaint and suggests how it might be resolved. The member state is given a time limit to submit its reply and if this is not forthcoming, or if the Commission is not satisfied with the response, proceedings may be commenced before the Court. The emphasis during this administrative phase of the procedure is on settling the problem by mutual agreement and if at any stage the Commission is satisfied that the member state concerned intends to comply with its ruling the infringement procedure may be suspended or closed. The issue only goes to the Court as a last resort. Article 186 allows the Commission or another party to a case before the Court to apply for interim measures which would prevent the defendant from continuing the infringement while the case was heard.

Article 171 states that:

> If the Court of Justice finds that a Member State has failed to fulfil an obligation under this Treaty, the State shall be required to take the necessary measures to comply with the judgment of the Court of Justice.

There was no power of enforcement in the original Treaty: compliance with Court judgments depended on moral suasion and the willingness of national courts to apply Community law. If an individual was aggrieved by a member state's failure to respect a judgment of the ECJ, he would have a remedy in the national courts.[9] This however was at best uncertain and with the volume of European legislation expanding rapidly as a result of the Single Market Programme, there was a danger that non-compliance would undermine the whole system. The Treaty of European Union (TEU) introduced an addition to Article 171 which enables the Commission to issue a further reasoned opinion if it considers that a member state has failed to comply with a judgment. If the necessary action is still not taken, the Commission may propose that the state be fined and the Court may then impose a penalty. The power to fine sovereign states for non-compliance with its decisions is a considerable enhancement of the Court's authority; all the more surprising that the British negotiators at Maastricht were among its most enthusiastic advocates.

Article 173 provides for the ECJ to review the legality of acts of the Council and Commission, and if necessary annul them 'on grounds of lack of competence, infringement of an essential procedural requirement, infringement of the Treaty or of any law relating to its application or misuse of powers.'

Subsequent judgments have widened the definition of 'acts' to cover any action by any of the institutions, including the European Parliament, 'which are binding on the applicant by bringing about a distinct change in his legal position.'[10] Indeed the European Parliament itself may bring an action where its powers and privileges are at issue, and an amendment to Article 173, as a result of the TEU, makes acts of the Parliament liable to judicial review if they produce legal effects. Natural and legal persons are entitled to bring an action where a decision by one of the institutions is specifically addressed to them or where a regulation or decision is of direct and individual concern to them.

Article 175 permits the member states and other institutions of the Community to complain to the Court that the Council or Commission have infringed the Treaty by failing to act after being called upon to do so. The TEU specifically extended this article to actions brought by the European Parliament as well as by the Council and Commission. As long ago as 1983 the Parliament had brought a successful action against the Council for failing to implement the Common Transport Policy required by Article 75 though the effect of the judgment was limited by the requirement that the obligations on the Council should be set out in specific terms. Natural and legal persons can use the Article 175 procedure only if the act that should have been passed would have been directly addressed to them.

One of the distinctive features of the ECJ's jurisdiction is the preliminary rulings procedure established by Article 177. This allows national courts or tribunals to refer questions affecting:

(a) the interpretation of this Treaty;
(b) the validity and interpretation of acts of the institutions of the Community;
(c) the interpretation of the statutes of bodies established by the Council, where those statutes so provide.

The purpose of this Article is to ensure that European law is interpreted in the same manner in all the member states so that it is a coherent system. The national Court requests the ECJ to explain what the law is, but retains the responsibility to apply that law to the facts of the case. Thus in the Factortame case, the ECJ declared that the domestic legislation was incompatible with Community law, but the national court carried out the review of the statute and provided the remedy. For this reason questions to the ECJ must be framed as general questions of law and not as a request for a judgment on the facts of a particular case. Whether to apply for a preliminary ruling is at the discretion of the national court, except in cases where no appeal is possible from its decision. Even then reference is not required if the point has been clearly resolved by a previous case.

Article 178 gives the Court jurisdiction over actions for non-contractual liability where, according to Article 215, the Community is liable to make good any damage caused by its institutions or by its servants in the performance of their duties. The most celebrated instance of this was the Adams case.[11] Stanley Adams informed the Commission that his employer, the Swiss firm La Roche, was in breach of competition policy, and provided documentary evidence. In the course of its investigations the Commission handed over some of these documents to the company from which they were able to identify Adams as the informant. He was arrested, charged with economic espionage and sentenced to a year's imprisonment, his business failed and he was bankrupted. The Court found that the Commission had been wrong to return the documents to La Roche and should have warned Adams that he faced prosecution if he returned to Switzerland. He was awarded substantial damages, but these were halved on the grounds that he had contributed to his own misfortunes.

In recent years the Court has taken a progressive view of Article 164 in the belief that it confers a general duty to create new areas of jurisdiction where necessary so as to ensure that the law is observed in the application and interpretation of the Treaties. It is this innovating role and the suspicion that the frontiers of European law are constantly being pushed outwards by a Court that is federal in its instincts that so concerns those who believe in the paramountcy of the nation-state. This is particularly the case where decisions of the Court seem to fly in the face of established national policy. Two 1980s cases illustrate the point.

The Marshall case[12] involved a nurse employed by the South West Area Health Authority who was compulsorily retired when she was over sixty, the age at which women qualified for pensions, but under sixty-five, which was the qualifying age for men. She brought an action before an employment tribunal contending that this was discriminatory because she was precluded from qualifying for the full male pension. The Court of Appeal asked the ECJ for a preliminary ruling as to whether this contravened the Equal Treatment Directive[13] and if so whether she could rely on this in an action against her employer. The Court ruled that although social security questions and therefore qualifying ages for pension were excluded from the operation of Article 5 (1) of Directive 76/20, the overriding point was that the plaintiff had been dismissed by the Health Authority solely because she had passed the pensionable age for women and this amounted to discrimination, so that the deliberate exclusion of social security matters from the directive was inoperative. The Court further held that the wording of Article 5 (1) of the Equal Treatment Directive was sufficiently clear and unambiguous as to have direct effect in the United Kingdom, in spite of the fact that it had not been implemented by a UK Statute and was in conflict with domestic law. It rejected the respondent's case that whereas the directives could be enforced against member states as such, it could not be enforced against them in their capacity as employers, subject, like private employers, to the domestic law. The ECJ pointed out that the difficulty would not arise if the directive had been properly implemented, and the government could not take advantage of its failure to do so.

The second case, *Barber* v. *Guardian Royal Exchange*,[14] finally established that pensions are to be considered as pay and therefore governed by Article 119 of the Treaty, which establishes the principle that men and women should receive equal pay for equal work. Mr Barber was a member of an occupational pension scheme in which the pensionable age was 65 for men and 60 for women. In the event of redundancy, men were entitled to an immediate pension at age 55 and women at 52. Barber was made redundant at 52 and received a cash benefit which was inferior to the pension he would have received had he been female. The Court of Appeal referred the case to the ECJ for a preliminary ruling and the Court declared that Article 119 applied with direct effect to occupational pension schemes where the beneficiary had 'contracted out', although in this case it held that the rule only took effect from the date of the judgment and therefore was only retrospective if plaintiffs had already commenced legal action. This limitation was confirmed by a Protocol to the TEU.

Whatever view one takes of the merits of the Marshall and Barber cases, both of which were regarded as triumphs for the cause of equal treatment, they raise important questions about the desirability of the ECJ's power to apply the general rules of the Treaty in a way that can so radically affect important areas of economic activity in the member states. Pensions legislation has now been changed as a result of the Marshall case in a way that the British Parliament left to itself would hardly have contemplated. In fact rather than reducing the pensionable to age to 60 for both men and women it has been raised to 65 which has serious implications for women who might wish to retire earlier. The Barber case could have meant that thousands of occupational pension schemes would have had to be revised at a cost running into billions of pounds in unfunded benefits. The effect could well have been to bankrupt the pensions industry with grave consequences for social stability. The TEU Protocol removed this possibility but nonetheless the entire pensions industry has had to change to conform with a principle established by a supranational court. It is reasonable to ask whether it is right that decisions of such magnitude should be made in this way without any reference to the national legislature, producing effects which are contrary to the declared policy of the elected government. These decisions beg the question whether this kind of social engineering, however well intentioned and justifiable, does not go far beyond the intentions of those who signed the original Treaties and indeed whether Treaty language was ever intended to be construed in this way.

Looking ahead to a European Union of 20 or more member states with very different legal systems and judicial traditions, the question arises whether the present Treaty articles are sufficient to sustain a satisfactory legal system. At very least consideration needs to be given to providing some form of appeal from decisions of the ECJ, perhaps to a superior court composed of senior judges of the national courts, which could act as a restraint on the federalist bias in the present system. There is something profoundly undemocratic in the prospect of a federal European Union being based on decisions of appointed judges rather than elected representatives and this raises questions as to the nature of the mandate for the revolutionary changes that the ECJ seems ready to espouse, interpreting Treaty provisions in a way that the original drafters could never have foreseen.

BIBLIOGRAPHY

In preparing this chapter I have relied heavily on Wyatt and Dashwood's *European Community Law*, third edition, published by Sweet & Maxwell in 1993. Other useful sources are: Bernard Rudden, *Basic Community Cases*, Clarendon Press, 1987, Neil Nugent, *The Government and Politics of the European Community*, second edition, Macmillan, 1991, and Josephine Shaw, *European Community Law*, Macmillan Professional Masters, 1993.

6 The Road to Maastricht: Turning point or turning back?

As the second Delors Commission took office in January 1989, the President could look back on his first four-year term with considerable satisfaction. The 1992 Single Market Programme had given the Community a new sense of direction and purpose and thanks to the work of Commissioner Lord Cockfield, was moving ahead at impressive speed. Spanish and Portuguese accession had been successfully completed and their adaptation to the EC structure had gone remarkably smoothly; the problem of the Community's finances had been resolved at least on a temporary basis and the interinstitutional agreement of 1987 had put an end to the unseemly wrangles over the budget that had debilitated the Community in the first part of the eighties. It was true that there had been no serious progress on the social front and reform of the Common Agricultural Policy continued to elude the Council of Agricultural Ministers, but the Single European Act (SEA) with its emphasis on majority voting had given renewed weight to Community decision-making, and the foundations for further integration and a more united Europe were well and truly laid. Jacques Delors himself was regarded as something of a miracle-worker; his renomination had proceeded without demur, and although something of a bogyman to the British, elsewhere he was regarded as the leading European statesman of the day, a man whose intellectual power and sense of mission made him the equal of any head of government.

This self-confidence was reflected in the President's speech presenting the new Commission to the European Parliament on 17 January 1989.

> . . . moves towards establishing a unified economic and social area are irreversible, and the Community has now set its sights on economic and monetary union, an ambition whose

very nature places it at the crossroads of economic integration and political union.

The revival of the Community, through the implementation of all the objectives of the Single Act has changed hearts and minds and given Europeans back their self confidence . . . The changes under way in Central and Eastern Europe combined with the faster integration of the Community, mean that Europeans can now aspire to heal the split in the old continent and give all its peoples the right of self determination. Little by little, Europe will once again take on the shape it has had throughout its history. Well beyond the Community there is a European blueprint for a society based on the principles of pluralism, democracy and the rule of law which the Community hopes will make headway in every part of Europe.

The reference to Eastern Europe was prompted by the rapid progress of liberalization in the Soviet Union and its satellites under Mikhail Gorbachev, whose standing in the eyes of Western public opinion rivalled that of Jacques Delors himself. The Soviet Army was withdrawing from Afghanistan, disarmament talks in Geneva and Vienna were showing signs of real progress, and the EC was engaged in trade talks with a superpower which until recently had refused even to acknowledge its existence. No one in January 1989 could have foreseen the speed at which the Soviet Empire was to collapse, as one satellite after another regained its freedom of action, culminating with the dissolution of the Soviet Union itself at the end of 1992. It was like a bicycle running downhill, slowly at first but gathering momentum and then as the brakes prove incapable of containing the speed, an irresistible headlong rush to a disintegrating crash at the bottom. All this lay in the future; as the new Commission took office most people envisaged a slow process of liberalization, accompanied by balanced reductions in armaments and the creation of a mutual security system through the CSCE.

As far as the Community was concerned the main focus at the beginning of the year was on Economic and Monetary Union (EMU); just as the 1992 Single Market Programme had provided the dynamic for the successes of the 1985 Commission so EMU would drive its successor. Monetary Union, though not mentioned in the original Treaties, had long been on the Community agenda as a necessary step towards full integration, comparable in its effects to the original establishment of the customs union in 1957. At the Hanover Summit in June 1988, the European Council affirmed its commitment to EMU and set up a Committee of Central Bank Governors and monetary experts, chaired by President Delors, to 'study and propose concrete stages leading towards economic and monetary union.'[1] The Committee reported in April 1989 producing a blueprint for progress towards EMU which it characterized as the irrevocable locking of exchange rates followed rapidly by the replacement of national currencies by a single currency.

The Delors Committee identified three stages leading to the achievement of EMU. The first stage, to begin on 1 July 1990, involved the creation of a single financial area free of exchange controls and other obstacles to the movement of funds with all member states joining the EMS. Stage 2 would involve the establishment of the basic organs and structures of EMU, in particular the European System of Central Banks, and Stage 3 would see the irrevocable locking of exchange rates which would herald full economic and monetary union. The Delors report was highly controversial both in its technical aspects, which many felt were too bureaucratic and prescriptive, and politically in that it clearly represented a massive advance in the process of European integration. Margaret Thatcher, who had signalled her opposition to federalism in the Bruges speech in September 1988, was critical on both counts, though her hostility probably had the effect of rallying her partners behind Delors. Moreover both the Foreign Secretary, Sir Geoffrey Howe, and the Chancellor of the Exchequer, Nigel Lawson, had come to the conclusion that Britain could not afford indefinitely to remain outside the ERM and be seen as blocking progress to monetary union. Their combined weight was sufficient to pressure Mrs Thatcher to agree to set conditions for Sterling's entry into the ERM; these had to be agreed at the Madrid Summit in June 1989 if Stage 1 was to get under way in time to fulfil the Delors Committee's timetable.

The Madrid conditions, as they came to be known, involved the removal of all exchange controls, the completion of the Single Market in Financial Services and strengthening competition policy.

'If these conditions are met,' declared the British Prime Minister, 'and provided inflation in the UK has been brought down significantly, the conditions would clearly exist to bring the pound into the Exchange Rate Mechanism.'

She went on to attack roundly the thinking behind Stages 2 and 3, observing with considerable prescience that the degree of transfer of national sovereignty over economic and monetary policy that they involved would be unacceptable to the British Parliament. The system proposed lacked accountability, and she doubted whether it would be acceptable to European public opinion. Other options should be explored and she undertook to table an alternative British approach.[2]

Little of this appeared in the Presidency's conclusions; the European Council restated its determination to achieve EMU as agreed at the Hanover Summit, accepted the Delors Report with some reservations and decided that Stage 1 would indeed commence on 1 July 1990. The Council and Commission were requested to adopt the legislation necessary to implement the co-ordination of economic policy required for Stage 1 and to carry out 'the preparatory work for the organization of an inter-governmental conference to lay down the subsequent stages; that conference would meet once the first stage had begun ...' The countdown to Maastricht had begun.

The Madrid Summit marks a watershed in the history of the Thatcher Government. There is no doubt that the Prime Minister was forced by her two senior colleagues into accepting the Madrid conditions against all her natural instincts. In July Sir Geoffrey Howe was removed from the Foreign Office to be replaced by John Major, and perhaps more significantly the relationship between the Prime Minister and her Chancellor was ruptured and never recovered. From then on the occupants of 10 and 11 Downing Street seemed to be pursuing different monetary policies, the one determined to stay out of the ERM and the other to join it. This was a major factor in Nigel Lawson's own resignation the following year and thus indirectly the fall of Mrs Thatcher herself in November 1991.

Margaret Thatcher is an instinctive nationalist who never felt comfortable with Britain's membership of the European Community. A teenager during the Second World War, she had been brought up to believe that the Germans were the enemy and France the ally who had let us down; by contrast the Americans were our staunch friends and allies who spoke our language and shared our culture. The Prime Minister had no sympathy for the grandiloquent declarations and high-flown idealism which are the natural currency of the Community and its institutions. She failed to realize that they were a necessary cloak for the day-to-day dealings of sovereign governments, each bent on pursuing their national interest, but accepting the need to do so within a collective framework. Time after time she signed up to Community Declarations, dismissing them as mere words, only to find subsequently that they involved commitments which would come back to haunt her.[3] She may even have thought that the others would never be able to meet the Madrid conditions, which involved finally ending controls on free movement of capital. In this she was certainly encouraged by some of her officials; contempt for foreigners is deeply engrained in the British establishment, ever since Bretherton withdrew from Messina, 'They'll never get their act together,' has been a constant refrain of British civil servants when contemplating a new Community initiative. Against this background Margaret Thatcher made the fundamental mistake of allowing her prejudices to cloud her judgement and seriously underestimated her partners, or as she would have termed them, opponents.

She never forgot the way in which she had been patronized by President Giscard and Chancellor Schmidt at the beginning of her premiership, or how by fighting her corner and refusing to give in she had forced the others to remedy the injustice of the British budget contribution. The tragedy is that having seen these tactics succeed once, she thought the trick could be repeated, failing to recognize that the other heads of government simply could not afford to let this happen again. Europe's leaders had too many memories of how the Community had nearly been destroyed by de Gaulle's obstructiveness in 1965 to allow one of their number to achieve a dominant position with the power to coerce the rest. Even when they might have agreed with Mrs Thatcher they could not afford to let her win. On her side she failed to appreciate that Jacques Delors, Helmut Kohl and François Mitterrand believed just as passionately in their vision of European Union as she did in the primacy of the nation-state: patriotism and conviction were not confined to one side of the Channel.

The pattern of her dealings with her fellow heads of government increasingly became one of bluster, followed inevitably by concessions which were so grudging and ungracious that they called in question Britain's commitment to the enterprise as a whole. Back home the press and media were quick to spot the popular appeal of anti-Europeanism, and were deliberately encouraged to run knocking stories by members of the Prime Minister's entourage; the seeds of destructive Euroscepticism were well and truly sown and a generation of young Conservative politicians were brought up to believe that Eurobashing was a certain passport to fame and fortune. It is ironic that at a time when the economic and political ideas associated with Thatcherism were breaking the mould in Britain and establishing a new orthodoxy in the West, their progenitor lacked the statesmanship and the magnanimity necessary to assume the leadership of the Community and secure her place in history as one of the great architects of European construction. That honour goes to Jacques Delors.

Economic and Monetary Union had been a long-standing feature of the European agenda; although controversial, the issues were understood and had been debated in Community circles ever since the Werner report of 1969. When the Intergovernmental Conference finally convened, the EMU topic had been thoroughly prepared and the basic questions were clear. The same could not be said for the parallel negotiations on political union; although this had featured in the Stuttgart Declaration in 1983 and in the preamble to the SEA, it had not attracted much attention during the period of the first Delors Commission and the issues that it raised had been discussed only in the vaguest terms. The expression Political Union was open to all kinds of misconstruction. The British chose to believe that it meant the immediate establishment of a federal superstate which involved the surrender of national sovereignty to a United States of Europe,[4] whereas for France and Germany it was a means of binding the Germans more deeply into a collective system and preventing them from using their economic power and geographical position to establish a European hegemony. Some of the smaller states such as Belgium and Holland believed it provided the means of preserving their influence and independence; others, Spain, Ireland and Greece, thought that it would reinforce solidarity and provide a framework for the fiscal transfers which would finance their economic development.

Political Union moved to the top of the Community agenda because of the extraordinary events of 1989, a year whose significance should rank with 1789, 1848 and 1914 in the annals of European history. At the beginning of the year Europe was still divided into the two blocs created by the post-war settlement; there had been substantial and welcome progress in the arms negotiations and signs of further rapprochement with conclusion of the successful CSCE follow-up negotiations in Stockholm. There were grounds for cautious optimism that Mikhail Gorbachev, 'a man we can do business with', would build a kinder and gentler version of the Soviet Union, based on the principles of glasnost and perestroika. By the end of the year the trickle of optimism had been transformed into a tidal wave of unstoppable change. First Poland and then Hungary and Czechoslovakia were permitted to detach themselves from the Soviet hegemony; the Warsaw Pact crumbled away leaving NATO intact and triumphant after 40 years of the Cold War. Hard-line Communist heads of government were replaced by liberals and throughout central and eastern Europe citizens' movements sprang up demanding civil rights and democratic elections. In the Baltic States and other long forgotten corners of the Soviet Empire nationalist movements acquired a new self-confidence and talk of independence became commonplace. In East Germany the Honecker regime was toppled after the local Red Army commander, taking instructions from Moscow, refused to use Soviet troops to disperse anti-government demonstrators. Then on 9 November the Berlin Wall, that symbol of the division of East and West, was breached and the reunification of Germany, which had been an impossible pipe-dream for two generations of Germans, suddenly became an imminent reality.

Once it became clear throughout central and eastern Europe that the Soviets no longer had the economic means or the political will to maintain their tutelage, people everywhere rose up and reasserted their independence. It was a popular revolution, which no statesman had predicted and none had the remotest idea how to handle.[5]

Statesmen and diplomats are obliged to affect a certain omniscience: people after all expect someone to be in charge and know what they are doing. In reality the process of government and international politics is largely reactive, with governments having to respond to a chain of unforeseen and unforeseeable events, many of them the unlooked-for results of their own previous decisions. Even before the Wall came down there had been substantial emigration from East to West Germany via the open Hungarian border, indeed the migrating family with their possessions piled precariously in their 'Trabbies' was a folk image for the times. Once the Wall was down the rate of migration increased sharply, so that by January 1990 more than two thousand people a day were leaving their homes in the East and arriving in the West. The West German Basic Law granted to all of them full rights of citizenship, including access to housing and social security, which placed enormous strain on the generous West German benefits system. To make matters worse the migrants were predominantly from the professional classes and skilled workers who were the very people most needed if the East German economy was to be brought up to Western standards; the revolution had removed the entire governing elite and there was an evident danger of civil breakdown and economic collapse.

Faced with this crisis Helmut Kohl and the West German Government decided that if people were to be persuaded to remain in East Germany they had to be given the necessary political and economic inducements to stay. This meant rapid progress towards German unification following free elections which in turn required the abrogation of the German State Treaty and the withdrawal of the two million Soviet troops stationed in East Germany. The economic guarantee was to be given in the form of a one-for-one conversion of the Ost Mark for the Deutsche Mark, German Economic and Monetary Union to be consummated as soon as a Unification Treaty between the two governments was signed. As the pressures built the pace quickened, Chancellor Kohl's original Ten Point Plan produced in November 1989 was rapidly telescoped from three years to twelve months. By the end of the year he had concluded a bilateral agreement with President Gorbachev covering the phased withdrawal of Soviet forces from German territory in return for massive German credits, among other things to build accommodation in Russia for the returning troops. Negotiations to end the four-power status of Berlin which had been one of the enduring features of post-war Europe were rapidly reduced to a formality. Elections were held in East Germany in March and returned a Christian Democrat majority with a mandate to begin unification negotiations immediately.

The geographical position of Germany in the middle of the European landmass has given her a pivotal role in the history of the Continent. The German question in different forms has dominated European politics since the time of the Emperor Augustus and the defeat of the Roman legions under Varus by Arminius. The post-war division of Germany was widely regarded as a safety measure preventing her from reasserting herself as she had done in the thirties; one of the factors behind the creation of the EC was the need to encompass Germany in a collective structure, removing the temptation to pursue her ambitions at the expense of her neighbours. Recent history has bred a deep distrust of German intentions and this in turn has made an indelible impression on the post-war generation of Germans. No one is more conscious of this than Helmut Kohl; in speech after speech he has made it clear that for his generation the European Community is the best guarantee of a peaceful Germany devoted to progress through common action:

> I feel carried back to an ill-fated past when I hear some people stirring up public sentiment with the argument that Germany has become too large and too powerful and therefore has to be 'contained' by means of coalitions. It is a cruel irony that such talk plays into the hands of just those forces in Germany which propagate an old style nationalism. Our answer to such short-sighted views is clear. The Federal Republic has made a final decision in favour of European integration.[6]

Political union for Kohl amounted to a guarantee that the European partners had nothing to fear from a newly united Germany so that the unification process could go ahead. For others it involved an affirmation of solidarity, a sign that Europeans intended to act together in preserving stability in an uncertain world.

A special meeting of the European Council took place in Dublin on 28 April 1990. Originally convened to consider the implications of German unification for the Community as a whole, it was manoeuvred by Germany and France into instructing the Foreign Ministers to prepare proposals for a second intergovernmental conference on political union to be held in parallel with that on EMU so that a new Treaty of Union could be ratified simultaneously with the Treaty on monetary union. This decision masked substantial differences of interpretation as to what political union would involve. Mrs Thatcher, with the support of smaller countries such as Holland, Denmark and Portugal, regarded it as a means of improving co-operation without any concessions of sovereignty, President Mitterrand favoured strengthening the Council of Ministers, while Chancellor Kohl preferred a more federal approach, extending majority voting and enhancing the role of the European Parliament. This confusion of aims was to last right through till the end of the IGC. The Dublin Summit also agreed the principles whereby a newly united Germany would become part of the European Community without Treaty amendment, a commitment that triggered off a remarkable legislative exercise which produced full integration in the EC on 1 January 1991.

Much of the problem with political union lay in the imprecise nature of the term itself. The various texts defining its content agreed by successive summits, reveal a somewhat prosaic plan to expand Community competences, notably over foreign and security policy, to improve decision-making by extending majority voting, making the legislative process more democratic by giving additional powers to the European Parliament and creating a sense of identity for its people by introducing a common citizenship. Much of the debate revolved round the eternal question of whether this could best be achieved by increasing the role and responsibilities of the supranational institutions or improving the mechanics of intergovernmental co-operation between the member states.

Following the Special Council there was a period of intense negotiation among the member states over what should be on the agenda of the Political Union IGC. The Foreign Ministers presented a paper to the regular European Council meeting in Dublin on 25–26 June 1990 which defined the objective as follows:

> To strengthen in a global and balanced manner the capacity of the Community and its Member States to act in the areas

of their common interests. The unity and coherence of its policies and actions should be ensured through strong and democratic institutions.

The paper then went on to list a series of questions: what further transfers of competence were required; how to extend the notion of a Community citizenship, based on freedom of movement and residence; whether to bring police and internal security measures within the Community framework. Each member state added favoured items to the menu; the British and their allies insisted on including a definition of what was not implied by political union and on arriving at a definition of subsidiarity which would guarantee its operational effectiveness. The Germans placed particular emphasis on increased involvement for the European Parliament including a role in the nomination of the president and members of the Commission, while the French, with British support, wanted national parliaments to be more involved in decisions on the transfer of competences. The second part of the paper, prompted by the Commission, set the stage for a review of the functioning of the institutions, including increased majority voting, and the final section covered the need for a Common Foreign and Security Policy, 'which takes account of the common interests of the Member States, acting with consistency and solidarity, and which institutionally goes beyond political cooperation as it currently functions.' The heads of government accepted this as the basis for the preparation of a second intergovernmental conference, to commence its work on 14 December and run in parallel with the one dealing with EMU which would open the day before. Both conferences were required to reach their conclusions in time for ratification of the resulting treaties to be completed before the end of 1992.

Preparation of the twin IGC's now passed to the Italians, traditionally among the most committed integrationists; they used a special summit at Rome on 27–28 October to isolate the British. Originally called to celebrate German unification which was achieved on 14 October, Prime Minister Andreotti, working closely with the Germans and French, produced a set of conclusions which pre-empted a great deal of the IGC agenda. With respect to EMU, 11 member states confirmed that the second stage would start on 1 January 1994 provided certain objective conditions were met, and undertook that steps to implement the third stage would begin within three years of the start of Stage 2. The British dissociated themselves from these conclusions, arguing that decisions on the substance of further moves towards EMU should precede decisions on timing. This not unreasonable objection took no account of the Community method, originated by Jean Monnet, which was to establish general goals, agree a deadline for achieving them and agree the details within this pre-set time-frame.

On Political Union the Rome conclusions stated that the objectives of the IGC were:

— to transform the Community into a European Union by extending its powers to other supplementary sectors of economic integration which are essential for convergence and social cohesion.
— developing the European Parliament's role in the legislative sphere.
— defining European citizenship.
— a Common Foreign and Security Policy which would go beyond the present limits in regard to security.

The UK also reserved its position on all these points, described by Mrs Thatcher as 'a rag bag of proposals'. She was however completely on her own; her outspoken opposition to every aspect of the two IGCs merely had the effect of driving potential allies into the other camp.

In the post-summit press conference the Prime Minister's isolation became all the more apparent when she asserted that the single currency proposals would never be accepted by the British Parliament and therefore would be vetoed. In her report to the House of Commons on 31 October, she rejected the suggestion of more powers for the European Parliament and other institutions with a ringing cry of 'No! No! No!' and seemed clearly to be heading for a split of de Gaulle type proportions with the European partners. It was this that precipitated the departure of the Deputy Prime Minister, Sir Geoffrey Howe, whose resignation speech in the House of Commons began the sequence of events that led to Mrs Thatcher's downfall. When the final summit of the year met in Rome, Margaret Thatcher was out of office and John Major was Prime Minister.

The Rome Summit which inaugurated the parallel IGCs was a little like Hamlet without the Prince. In deference to the new

British Prime Minister, the final list of topics to be covered by the IGC on political union was less prescriptive than before and certain issues which were important to the UK such as consensus in shaping the guidelines for a Common Foreign and Security Policy, increased powers on budgetary control and financial accountability, and a role for national Parliaments were given increased emphasis. As the Prime Minister put it at his press conference: 'We have a menu for the IGC, our favourite dishes are on that menu, so are others favourite dishes, but the Community has not decided what orders to place.'

It seemed that a more conciliatory style had proved a more effective way of fighting Britain's corner.

The first part of 1991 was overshadowed by the Gulf War and the increasing tension in the former Yugoslavia, both of which posed questions about the Community's ability to act decisively and with effect. The main issue in the conference on political union was the extent to which the Commission would be involved in new areas of competence such as foreign affairs and internal security. President Delors through his deputy chef de cabinet, François Lamoreux, pushed for a solution that would have given the Commission equal status with the governments in these areas. The British were determined to resist this and also to ensure that the jurisdiction of the Court of Justice should not be extended beyond the existing Treaties.

The June Summit in Luxembourg saw the tabling of a draft treaty by the Presidency which was accepted as forming the basis for further negotiations. However, many important questions were left unresolved, notably the decision-taking procedure in the CFSP, defence policy, the powers of the European Parliament, qualified majority voting, additional competences and strengthening the social dimension. There were dark mutterings about British obstruction and the heads of government found it easier to identify areas where they disagreed than any common ground though there was a welcome for a German paper outlining the aims of the IGC as regards common action on home affairs and judicial policy. This included immigration policy, police co-operation, and joint action against drug trafficking, terrorism and other forms of international crime which were eventually to be included in the third pillar of the Maastricht Treaty.

The main issue affecting EMU concerned the degree of

convergence between the national economies that was necessary before Stage 3 could be initiated and how it would be
measured. Jacques Delors said at his press conference that
agreement still had to be reached on the role of the Ecu, the
content of Stage 2 and the budgetary constraints to be imposed
on member states who were part of the system. This reflected
growing German fears that improvident southern countries
such as Greece would use the German currency reserves to
finance their swelling budget deficits.

The decisive moment came in September when the Dutch
Presidency, led by their junior Foreign Minister Piet Dankert,
former President of the European Parliament, produced proposals which went far further in terms of powers for the Commission and the European Parliament than the majority of
their partners were prepared to contemplate. The Dutch proposals were decisively rejected and the member states agreed
to return to the more cautious Luxembourg draft. The British
position that the new areas of CFSP and Justice and Home
Affairs should be intergovernmental gained ground and the
ambitions of the Commission and its President received a
substantial check. The remaining period of negotiation was
devoted to identifying those questions which would have to be
resolved by the European Council itself when it convened at
Maastricht on 9 December.

The Summit meeting was intense and hard fought, indeed
it seemed for a time that no agreement would be reached and
the IGCs would be seen to have failed. In the end the heads of
government were able to reach a consensus but at the considerable price of two British opt-outs which breached the hitherto sacrosanct principle of Community solidarity; that is that
once agreement has been reached the Community acts as one.
The first opt-out, which allowed the UK to postpone its decision
on whether to join EMU until the end of 1996 or 1998, had
been implicit in the negotiations ever since the special Rome
Summit in October 1990 when the UK Government had reserved its position; however Britain was to remain part of the
process and would play a full part in establishing EMU even
though she was not committed to join. The second opt-out
from the Social Chapter of the Treaty was much more problematic. The Conservative Government had a long history of
blocking Community initiatives in the sphere of social policy

and had refused to sign up to the Social Charter in 1989. The assumption had been that, in addition to the EMU opt-out, enough concessions had been made on the role of the institutions and the intergovernmental character of Common Foreign and Security Policy and Justice and Home Affairs and their exclusion from the established structure of the Treaties, to persuade the UK to swallow the Social Chapter and maintain Community solidarity. In the event this was not enough and John Major made it clear that if Britain was required to accept the social provisions he would veto the agreement as a whole. Rather than see the negotiations collapse the Germans and French accepted a solution whereby 11 member states accepted the Social Chapter, which was annexed to the Treaty as a protocol. When the British Prime Minister described his negotiating success as 'Game, Set and Match', he was not far from the truth. The UK had succeeded in dictating the shape of the new Treaty at very little apparent political cost. Assuming that it was not her wish to detach herself from the European mainstream, Maastricht was the best deal that could have been struck.

The Treaty of European Union (TEU), which was agreed at Maastricht on 11 December 1990, and signed the following February, describes itself as 'marking a new stage in the process of creating an ever closer union in which decisions are taken as closely as possible to the citizen.' Title 1 sets out the objectives of the Union which include economic and social progress,[7] asserting its international identity, introduction of citizenship of the Union, close cooperation in justice and home affairs and to maintain the *acquis communautaire*. The Union has a single institutional framework comprising three independent pillars, the European Community (EC) itself which includes EMU, the Common Foreign and Security Policy (CFSP), and Cooperation in the fields of Justice and Home Affairs (JHA). The European Council is responsible for providing the necessary impetus for the development of the Union defining general political guidelines, the Council and Commission are charged with ensuring the consistency of Union policies. The traditional institutional structure only applies to the first pillar, the other two are intergovernmental with the Council as the principal actor; in particular they are excluded from the jurisdiction of the Court of Justice.

The third pillar, cooperation in the fields of Justice and Home affairs, is covered by Title VI of the Treaty. The areas described as being of common interest are asylum policy, controls at external frontiers, immigration, co-operation in combating drug addiction and fraud, judicial co-operation in civil and criminal matters, customs and police co-operation.[8] Law and order and internal security are specifically reserved for the member states. The Council may, following an initiative from a member state or the Commission in the case of civil matters only, draw up joint positions, adopt joint actions and prepare conventions which it recommends to member states for adoption according to their internal procedures. The Council is supported by a Coordinating Committee of senior officials, analogous to COREPER which may deliver opinions and prepare Council decisions. These may provide for implementing measures to be adopted by majority vote, otherwise unanimity is the rule. The Commission is to be fully associated with these activities and the European Parliament has the right to be regularly informed and to ask questions.

It is clear that these arrangements for the third pillar which are similar in character to those of the second are far removed from the conception of the Community established by the original Treaty of Rome. Far from being an equal partner with the Council, the Commission is reduced to the status of an observer, the Coordinating Committee is made up of national as opposed to Community officials and decisions on majority voting are taken ad hoc, with no Treaty-based procedure being laid down. The Parliament and the Court are mere onlookers and the Court has no jurisdiction unless invited. The JHA pillar is a loose-knit international organization, similar to the OECD, with only limited powers to bind its members. This represents a major setback for federalism: the idea of a single European Government at best lies far in the future. Taken together with the UK opt-out from the Social Chapter which drives a coach and horses through the principle of Community solidarity, these arrangements represent a sea change in the nature of the Community, a significant turning away from the original vision of a united Europe. If the European Union continues on the path charted at Maastricht the loose association of sovereign states which Margaret Thatcher visualized at Bruges in 1988 is likely to become the pattern.

By the same token Maastricht was a serious defeat for Jacques Delors and the Commission: they had hoped to repeat the experience of the 1986 IGC and the Single European Act when the Commission had dominated the agenda and thus consolidated and extended its influence. In 1989 EMU had been selected as the next dynamic idea to drive the Community forward, creating the momentum for closer political integration to follow. However the break-up of the Soviet Empire and the turmoil in Yugoslavia destabilized the situation and the Commission lost control of events. The Commission worked doggedly within the IGCs to deliver a federal agenda, but a combination of British resistance and German preoccupation with instability on its borders weakened its credibility and undermined its influence. The Commission lost at Maastricht because despite its pretensions it was not a European government.

Although the TEU marks a significant turning away from federalism it has not resolved the issue of how Europe will be governed in future. Intergovernmentalism may have triumphed, but it has yet to be shown that it can provide answers to the problems of a divided continent. Progress in the second and third pillars has been extremely limited and the member states find it as difficult as before to take the decisions that matter. There is a real possibility that if the Maastricht pillars fail to produce concrete results, a hard core of states may decide to revert to the original treaties and create an inner union within a much larger association of states, going back to something very like the Europe of the original six. As far as the larger Union is concerned, Maastricht marks a decisive turning away from the ideals of the Founding Fathers, but it may yet prove the point at which some of the member states set out on a course towards a true federal union while others jump ship. The Maastricht Summit was most certainly a turning point; it is not yet clear however whether it marked a final turning back.

7 The Competences of the Union: Centralism or subsidiarity?

The Maastricht negotiations introduced the concept of a three-pillared structure for the European Union[1] of which the European Community with its unique structure of supranational institutions was one. The other two, Common Foreign and Security Policy and Internal Security, are intergovernmental in their nature and outside the jurisdiction of the Court of Justice. The European Community proper, the first pillar, is concerned largely with economic matters, and its competences, that is those areas where it has powers to act, have been extended well beyond that which was envisaged in the original Treaty of Rome. However, the principle of subsidiarity as set out in Article 3b is intended as a constraint on the use of its powers by stipulating that the Community can only act where the common objective cannot be achieved by member states acting on their own.

> The Community shall act within the limits of the powers conferred upon it by this Treaty and of the objectives assigned to it therein.
> In areas which do not fall within its exclusive competence, the Community shall take action according to the principle of subsidiarity, only if and in so far as the objectives of the proposed action cannot be sufficiently achieved by the Member States and therefore by reason of the scale and effects of the proposed action, be better achieved by the Community. Any action by the Community shall not go beyond what is necessary to achieve the objectives of this Treaty.

This Article was designed to put a ring fence round the European Community and prevent the supranational institutions from further extending their powers at the expense of the member states. In this respect it reverses the original Treaty of Rome, which foresaw a rapid accumulation of power at the centre with the consent of the member states represented in the Council. Article 3b is the response of the national governments to fears of excessive centralization leading to the establishment of a superstate which were voiced by Margaret Thatcher at Bruges; it remains to be seen how effective it will be. The history of the Community suggests that its ability to extend its competences is directly related to its ability to build up public support for its ambitions. In the eighties the 1992 Single Market Project attracted widespread support, particularly in the business community and this enabled the Commission to drive the sometimes reluctant governments along the path to integration, guided by a common objective. By contrast the failure to rally a similar degree of support for monetary union and political union in the early nineties put the Commission on the defensive, echoing a widespread loss of confidence in European solutions to the problems that people encountered in their daily lives. If the Community were to recapture the public imagination and rally support for a new common objective, subsidiarity would not be an obstacle; as things are it provides some reassurance that centralization will not be able to go too far.

The tasks of the European Community (EC), that is the first of the three pillars of the European Union, are defined in Article 2 of the new EC Treaty as follows:

> The Community shall have as its task, by establishing a common market and an economic and monetary union and by implementing the common policies and activities referred to in Articles 3 and 3a, to promote throughout the Community a harmonious and balanced development of economic activities, sustainable and non inflationary growth respecting the environment, a high degree of convergence of economic performance, a high level of employment and of social protection, the raising of the standard of living and quality of life and economic and social cohesion and solidarity among Member States.

This is a longer version of the article in the original Treaty and adds economic and monetary union as an objective as well as mentioning the environment, and economic and social cohesion, both modern and politically correct concerns. In this respect the new Treaty does add significantly to the Community's competences. Article 3 lists the activities associated with these objectives as follows:

(a) the elimination, as between Member States, of customs duties and quantitative restrictions on the import and export of goods, and of all other measures having equivalent effect;

(b) a common commercial policy;

(c) an internal market characterized by the abolition, as between Member States, of obstacles to the free movement of goods, persons, services and capital;

(d) measures concerning the entry and movement of persons in the internal market as provided for in Article 100c;[2]

(e) a common policy in the sphere of agriculture and fisheries;

(f) a common policy in the sphere of transport;

(g) a system ensuring that competition policy in the internal market is not distorted;

(h) the approximation of the laws of the Member States to the extent required for the functioning of the common market;

(i) a policy in the social sphere comprising a European Social Fund;

(j) the strengthening of economic and social cohesion;

(k) a policy in the sphere of the environment;

(l) the strengthening of the competitiveness of Community industry;

(m) the promotion of research and technological development;

(n) encouragement for the establishment and development of trans-European networks;

(o) a contribution to the attainment of a high level of health protection;

(p) a contribution to education and training of quality and to the flowering of the cultures of the Member States;

(q) a policy in the sphere of development co-operation;

(r) the association of overseas countries and territories in order to increase trade and promote jointly economic and social development;

(s) a contribution to the strengthening of consumer protection;

(t) measures in the spheres of energy, civil protection and tourism.

This is quite an impressive list; of these twenty explicit competences a, b, c, e, f, g, h, i, r are present in the original Article 3 of the Treaty of Rome, which was left unchanged by the Single European Act. The SEA contains chapters on economic and social cohesion, research and environment, but immigration policy, competitiveness, trans-European networks, health, education, development, and consumer protection are all new Treaty objectives. There had been activities in these areas before, using Article 235 which enables the Commission to introduce proposals to achieve the objectives of the Community where the Treaty has not provided the necessary powers as a legal base. To that extent the TEU recognized a situation that already existed rather than introducing anything very new. Everything not covered by Article 3 is reserved to the member states, if the Commission sought to introduce measures in these areas it would have to use Article 235, which requires the Council to be unanimous, so any extension of the Community's competences is subject to a national veto.

Previously many of the sectors that were recognized by treaty for the first time had been covered by measures introduced under Article 100 and later 100a. These are the Articles which cover harmonization of national rules, which was necessary to create the Single Market and in some cases at least the connection was rather tenuous. By extending the list of competences and consolidating what had already been achieved, the Maastricht negotiators have reduced the Commission's ability to interpret the Treaty creatively, so extending its field of activity.

The original Treaty established a consultation procedure with a single parliamentary reading; the Council merely consulted the European Parliament by asking for its opinion on a Commission proposal. The co-operation procedure introduced by the SEA, and now incorporated in Article 189c of the Treaty, added a second reading procedure. At this stage the European Parliament, acting by a majority of its members, could reject the Council's common position, established after the first reading, or retable amendments that the Council had rejected. The Council required unanimity to override rejection or to defeat Parliamentary amendments provided they were supported by the Commission.

The TEU established a third procedure, the conciliation procedure set out in Article 189b. This adds a third stage in the shape of a conciliation committee made up of an equal numbers of Council members and MEPs which considers parliamentary amendments adopted at the second reading. This is required to reach agreement by qualified majority of both sides, otherwise the Council itself needs a qualified majority to adopt the text and the European Parliament has an ultimate right to reject it.

Finally there is an assent procedure established by Article O of the TEU, which requires that the Parliament ratifies accession treaties by an absolute majority of its members. This also applies to proposals facilitating the free movement of citizens under Article 8a, the implementation of monetary policy (Article 105 (6)), and fixing the priorities of the structural funds.

As far as the present competences are concerned the Commission has complete responsibility for the Customs Union as regards the elimination of customs duties and quantitative restrictions between member states and for the implementation of Treaty rules on competition and state aids. The consultation procedure applies to agriculture, free movement of services, but not capital, rights of establishment, approximation of laws and industrial policy. The co-operation procedure (Article 189c) applies to transport, social policy, trans-European networks, implementation of the structural funds regulations, environment policy, and development and co-operation. The conciliation procedure (Article 189b) covers free movement of workers, education and training, culture, health, consumer protection, and research and technology. The ECOFIN Council retains untrammelled control over economic and monetary policy and taxation.

Generally speaking the more significant policies remain the province of the Commission and Council, with the Parliament playing at best a consultative role; economic and industrial questions, notably the approximation of laws under Article 100a which covers most single market legislation, are subject to the co-operation procedure giving the Parliament the role of an advisory and amending chamber, similar to the House of Lords. The new conciliation procedure applies to those areas which impact most obviously on the citizen, though in many cases they are relatively undeveloped. Where the Treaty requires unanimity in the Council the consultation procedure is sufficient, as all member states by definition must agree to the measure and therefore national parliaments retain some control; when majority voting is permitted, greater involvement by the European Parliament balances the possibility that one or more member states could be outvoted. How credible this is to the outside world is another question.

Although the democratic accountability of the Community has been enhanced by these changes they do not affect some of the most significant areas of policy and the procedures are so complicated as to be incomprehensible to the ordinary person. The Council continues to meet in secret and national Parliaments have no say in the legislative process; much more will need to be done before the Community can be said to be truly transparent and open to public scrutiny. This opacity is one·of the main causes of the crisis of public confidence which is undermining the European Union: few people understand what it does or how it operates and this widespread ignorance makes it vulnerable to rumour and misconstruction. In the eyes of its citizens the Union seems impenetrable, threatening and dull.

Title I of the Treaty, Articles 9–37, is concerned with the free movement of goods. The establishment of a customs union eliminating duties between member states was the principal objective of the original Treaty of Rome and finally completed in 1980. It remains one of the principal sources of Commission Regulations, which deal with the administration of the Common External Tariff and trade relations with third countries. Article 31 which prohibits member states from introducing quantitative restrictions on trade between themselves 'or measures having equivalent effect', is a potent source of complaints from industry against member states' attempts to protect their domestic markets; the Commission is bound to investigate these and if necessary use the Article 169 procedure to compel them to respect their obligations.

Title II, Articles 38–47, covers Agriculture. The Common Agricultural Policy was devised by the Dutch Commissioner

Sicco Mansholt in the late 1950s and was launched in 1963 when common prices for cereals were agreed between France and Germany. Article 39 defines the objectives of the CAP as follows:

(a) to increase agricultural productivity by promoting technical progress and by ensuring the rational development of agricultural production and the optimum utilisation of the factors of production, in particular labour;

(b) thus to ensure a fair standard of living for the agricultural community, in particular by increasing the individual earnings of persons engaged in agriculture;

(c) to stabilise markets;

(d) to assure the availability of supplies;

(e) to ensure that supplies reach consumers at reasonable prices.

Despite these unremarkable objectives the CAP has aroused the strongest passions across the Community ever since its inception. For farmers and their supporters it is the element that justifies the Community's existence, to others it is the epitome of waste and profligacy, a rip-off of consumers by vested interests. Adjectives such as 'obscene' and 'ludicrous' are freely bandied about in the tabloid press. In fact in its early years the CAP's system of border protection, guaranteed common prices and balancing markets through intervention worked very well. Self-sufficiency in food products was substantially increased and rural dereliction and a drift to the towns by impoverished peasants largely avoided. Unfortunately the Council of Agricultural Ministers, who control the CAP, proved quite incapable of agreeing on necessary reforms once the cost of agricultural support soared out of control in the early eighties. Unwilling to face down their domestic agricultural lobbies, the farm ministers offered a series of palliatives, co-responsibility, stabilizers, quantitative production ceilings, all of which they unpicked as soon as they were adopted, in an attempt to protect their own producers before the restraints on production started to bite. Every sector in every country became a special case. Those who believe that the Council of Ministers are best equipped to run the Community and that the Commission should be stripped of its right of initiative should be asked to explain how they square this with the constant criticism of the CAP in their press and media. Indeed it was the Commission which, in 1992, initiated the MacSharry reforms; support was shifted from product to incomes and the Community was able to reach an agreement with the Americans in the framework of the GATT Uruguay Round to reduce agricultural support progressively over a ten-year period. Taken together MacSharry and Uruguay have revolutionized the CAP, though it will be some time before the full impact of the reform makes itself felt.

Title III (Articles 48–73) covers freedom of movement of persons, services and capital. These, with free movement of goods, constitute the basic building blocks of the Single Market. The rights of workers to seek employment in any part of the Community and enjoy the same rights as the nationals of the country in which they find themselves is fundamental to the concept of a common market. The Treaty entitles citizens from other member states to full social security cover for themselves and their dependants, the right of establishment as self-employed professionals and to have their qualifications recognized. In this field in particular, Community citizenship confers important rights on the individual which are not available to citizens of third countries. Although the original Treaty focused on workers, the principle of free movement has been extended to cover any citizen, employed or not, who wishes to move from one country to another. Free movement of services and capital was enshrined in the original Treaty but was inoperative until the introduction of qualified majority voting following the Single European Act made it possible to introduce common standards and compatible regulatory systems.

Title IV (Articles 74–84) provides for a common transport policy. On the surface this is one of the most obvious areas for collective action: after all a common system of transport is essential if there is to be free movement of goods. Although common rules have gradually been introduced, member states have proved extremely reluctant to harmonize their national regulations. Matters have not been helped by the failure of the Council to make sufficient funds available in the Budget to finance large-scale infrastructure projects, thus depriving the Community of real bargaining power.

Title V (Articles 85–102) deals with common rules on competition, taxation and approximation of laws. In many ways this is the most significant part of the Treaty. Competition Policy covers concentrations, cartels and abuse of dominant positions as well as state aids and in these areas the Commission has almost total freedom of action. Over time it has developed its own system of anti-trust law which it can enforce with fines on offending enterprises. Recent examples include the cement industry, fibreboard manufacturers and the steel industry. Some of the biggest names including ICI and IBM have been the target of Commission investigators as they seek to prevent partitioning of markets and price fixing. A particularly controversial subject is state aids as they bring the Commission into direct conflict with those member states who seek to build up and protect privileged sectors of their national industry. It is here that the dichotomy between surrender of national sovereignty and the advantages of economic integration is at its most stark. An effective competition policy is just as important to the operation of the Single Market as common standards, but the Commission's record has been patchy. There have been many justified complaints at its failure to discipline the aids that some countries give to their airlines and electronics industries, as well as those that are used to prop up dying traditional industries such as steel, textiles and shipbuilding. The Competition Directorate, DG IV, has quasi-judicial powers, analogous to those of the Department of Trade and Industry in Britain, and it has been suggested that these would be better exercised by an independent body operating within the framework of the Court of Justice.

The taxation provisions forbid discriminatory taxation of goods in free circulation within the Single Market and provide for a common system of VAT. Article 99 requires unanimity for the adoption of measures harmonizing indirect taxes, thus preserving the paramountcy of the member states in this important area. Direct taxation is not covered by the Treaty.

Article 100a, introduced by the Single European Act, provides the legal base for the harmonization of standards required to achieve the Single Market. This is defined in Article 7b as follows:

> The internal market shall comprise an area without internal frontiers in which the free movement of goods, persons, services and capital is ensured in accordance with the provisions of this Treaty.

The establishment of common standards is essential if the free movement of goods and services is to be assured. Under Lord Cockfield's 'New Approach', framework directives establish general principles which are then implemented through national legislation, the standards themselves being agreed by independent committees of businessmen and trade experts. This is in contrast to the previous system by which the Commission itself tried to draw up detailed standards and carry them through the elaborate legislative process. Without the 'New Approach' there would be no Single Market.

Title VI (Articles 102a–109m) incorporates the agreements reached at Maastricht on Economic and Monetary Policy including the agreed steps to an Economic and Monetary Union and the constitution of a European Central Bank. This was one of the main achievements of the Maastricht Summit and will be covered separately in Chapter 10.

Title VII (Articles 110–116) deals with the common commercial policy. This is the external counterpart of the customs union and enables the Commission to undertake trade negotiations with third countries and in international fora such as the GATT on behalf of all member states. Article 113 allows the Commission to make recommendations to the Council for opening trade negotiations, and following authorization, conduct them on behalf of the Community as a whole in consultation with a Council committee. The negotiations in the Uruguay Round were conducted according to this procedure. There is no doubt that the Community's influence on the outcome of the Round was massively enhanced by there being one negotiator, Sir Leon Brittan, representing all 12 member states. The EC and the USA were able between them to determine the outcome, thus making an important contribution to a more open trading environment. Article 115 stipulates that any protective measures adopted by a member state must be approved by the Commission in advance. Parliament has a right to be informed of the process of trade negotiations, but no right to be consulted or to intervene, except where association agreements are being negotiated and the assent procedure is required by Article 228.

Title VIII (Articles 117–127) covers social policy, education, training and youth. Article 118 states that:

> ... the Commission shall have the task of promoting close
> co-operation between Member States in the social field par-
> ticularly in matters relating to:
> — employment
> — labour law and working conditions
> — basic and advanced vocational training
> — social security
> — prevention of accidents and diseases
> — occupational hygiene
> — the right of association and collective bargaining between
>   employers and workers.

However the Article only provides for making studies and issuing opinions; it does not include a right to initiate legislation.
This is covered by Article 118a which allows the co-operation
procedure to be used for measures to improve the working
environment and the health and safety of workers. One of
the major bones of contention with the British Government is
the way in which Article 118a has been used to introduce legislation on working conditions which go well beyond a strict
definition of health and safety.

Protocol 14 to the Treaty records that 11 member states
wish to continue along the path laid down in the 1989 Social
Charter and permits them to use the procedures of the Community for this purpose. Britain is not bound by this agreement, which is annexed to the Treaty, and incorporates the
additional articles that would have been part of the Treaty
itself had it been possible to reach agreement among 12
member states. The Social Chapter adds legislative teeth to
Article 118 and provides for the Social Partners, representing
employers and trade unions to be directly involved in the
legislative procedure. It remains to be seen how practicable
this device will prove.

Article 119 lays down the principle that men and women
should receive equal pay for equal work and has been subject
to much interpretation by the Court of Justice. Article 123
establishes the European Social Fund with the objective:

> to render the employment of workers easier and to increase
> their geographical and occupational mobility within the Com-
> munity, and to facilitate their adaptation to industrial changes

and to changes in production systems, in particular through vocational training and retraining.

The ESF, which nowadays comes under the umbrella of the Structural Funds, is thus concerned with training and development, not social security as its name might suggest.

Title IX, Culture, Title X, Public Health, and Title XI Consumer Protection all give Treaty status to areas which had been dealt with under Articles 100 and 235. Each now has an independent legal base within the Treaty and legislation can be introduced using the new conciliation procedure.

Title XII, another Maastricht innovation, establishes the concept of Trans-European Networks (TENs). These are cross-frontier links in the fields of transport, telecommunications and energy infrastructures which bind the economies of the member states more closely together and have the effect of drawing the peripheral regions of the Community closer to the centre. Examples of TENs include the Channel Tunnel, the undersea electricity cable that links Britain with France and enables French nuclear powered energy to be sold to British consumers, and cross-frontier telephone links.

Title XIII lays down the principles of an industry policy with the objectives of:

— speeding up the adjustment of industry to structural changes;
— encouraging an environment favourable to initiative and to the development of undertakings throughout the Community, particularly small and medium sized undertakings;
— encouraging an environment favourable to co-operation between undertakings;
— fostering better exploitation of the industrial potential of policies of innovation, research and technological development.

This is a good deal weaker than the more interventionist minded states and the Commission would have wished, and significantly legislation requires unanimity in the Council, which merely has to consult the European Parliament.

Title XIV, Economic and Social Cohesion, provides the basis for the operation of the Community's Structural Funds. The

European Regional Development Fund (ERDF) is the main instrument for promoting the development of the poorer member states and accounts for about 20 per cent of Community spending. Under the current Structural Fund Regulation, adopted in 1992, its main objectives are the development of the infrastructure in those regions where the GDP per capita is substantially below the Community average (Objective 1), assistance for areas of high unemployment where traditional industry is in structural decline (Objective 2). The European Social Fund (ESF)[3] finances training and measures to help the unemployed (Objective 3) and measures to avoid people becoming unemployed (Objective 4), and the guidance section of the European Agricultural Guidance and Guarantee Fund (EAGGF)[4] covers the improvement of agricultural structures and help for areas where high unemployment has resulted from agricultural decline (Objectives 5a and 5b).

The Cohesion Fund, established at Maastricht and implemented as a result of agreements at the 1992 Edinburgh Summit, provides finance for 'environmental projects and Trans-European Networks in the area of transport infrastructure'. Money from the Cohesion Fund is available for projects which involve the four poorest member states, Spain, Portugal, Greece and Ireland, and was their principal gain from the Maastricht process. The amount of money available was agreed as part of the overall financial package at the Edinburgh Summit in December 1992 and was an important element in the internal negotiations which enabled the accession negotiations with Austria, Finland, Sweden and Norway to be brought to a successful conclusion. Spain and the other poorer countries view the Cohesion Fund as compensation to them for the increased competition they will experience as a consequence of enlargement; there was a precedent in the shape of the Integrated Mediterranean Programmes (IMPS) which provided similar compensation to Southern Italy, Corsica and Greece at the time of Spanish and Portuguese accession in 1987. The size and role of the Cohesion Fund will certainly be a major factor in the negotiations for further enlargement to the East towards the end of the decade.

The framework regulations which set the objectives and implementing conditions for the Structural Funds are adopted for a period of five years using the co-operation procedure. The

new Committee of Regions composed of nominated representatives of regional and local government, which is established by the TEU, has the right to be consulted.

Title XV, Research and Technological Development, makes
provision for a multi-annual framework programme for research, which establishes the scientific and technological objectives to be achieved. This is adopted by the Council acting
unanimously using the conciliation procedure. Implementing
measures require a qualified majority and consultation; this
effectively prevents the Parliament from interfering in the detail of programmes. The research activities of the Commission
have long been a battlefield between those governments that
believe expensive programmes of state-sponsored research to
be the most effective way of maintaining Europe's technological competitiveness and those, like the British, that believe
these things are best left to private sector investment. In practice the research programmes have tended to be dominated by
a limited number of major companies who themselves provide
much of the cash.

Title XVI provides the basis for an environment policy with
the following characteristics:

— preserving, protecting and improving the quality of the
  environment;
— protecting human health;
— prudent and rational utilisation of natural resources;
— promoting measures at international level to deal with
  regional or worldwide environmental problems.

Legislation is by the co-operation procedure except for fiscal
measures, those involving planning, water resources, and the
general structure of energy supply: these require unanimity following a consultation procedure.

Title XVII covers Development and Co-operation. Until
Maastricht development policy had no treaty base, but was
dealt with as a substructure of the Common Commercial Policy
or within the framework of the Lome Convention, an international treaty concluded by the member states and the Commission independently of the EC. Article 130u now provides
a statement of objectives and Article 130w establishes a legal
base using the co-operation procedure.

As far as the European Community is concerned the TEU

is for the most part a matter of consolidating and codifying existing competences rather than creating new ones. Even the notion of citizenship in Article 8 is not really new, but provides a conceptual and legal framework for a number of existing rights; new rights that are created, the right to stand in elections and to diplomatic and consular protection, are of minor concern to the majority of citizens. The new areas of Union competence are to be found in the second and third pillars which have a different institutional structure. Although EMU is part of the European Union Treaty, it also has an independent character which is distinct from the framework of the original Treaties. The principal innovations are procedural – notably in the form of the conciliation procedure which marginally increases the powers of the European Parliament, and the creation of the Committee of Regions – and managerial, through the recognition of the Court of Auditors as a fully fledged institution and the enhancement of the power of the Court of Justice to enforce decisions.

The principal innovation is the emphasis on subsidiarity. As already pointed out this represents a fundamental shift in direction for the Community, the concept itself is imprecise and there are no rules for establishing how it will be decided when 'the objectives of a proposed action cannot be sufficiently achieved by the Member States' – presumably this is a question for ad hoc decisions by the European Council. This pattern of limiting common action to exceptional cases is reproduced in the second and third pillars and the general effect is to put strict limits on the further devolution of power to the centre through the creative interpretation of existing Treaty articles. It is not yet clear to what extent this will affect the Court of Justice's role in extending the frontiers of Community law.

Subsidiarity has fundamentally altered the blueprint for a united Europe set out in the Treaty of Rome but it has not altered the *acquis communautaire*, which remains intact. As a result the Community retains competences in significant areas of economic life where the member states have accepted that common action is in their interests. There are those who argue that some of these powers should be repatriated; they have never made it clear which powers they have in mind or how the collective interest would be served better if they were returned to the member states. As the current President of the

Commission, Jacques Santer, has said, 'The Community must concentrate on doing fewer things better',[5] and the Commission would certainly be wise to concentrate its efforts on using the present *acquis* effectively, and give a practical demonstration of the advantages of common action. It may well be that if the intergovernmental approach continues to be characterized by vacillation and drift people may once again turn to more federal solutions as the best way of fulfilling their political and economic needs.

8 The Common Foreign and Security Policy: 'The mouse that roared'

There is no reference to foreign policy co-ordination in the Treaty of Rome; no doubt the Founding Fathers felt that following the collapse of the European Defence Community in 1953 this was too sensitive an area for common action. Moreover the Cold War and the division of Europe into two armed camps remained the central geopolitical fact and attempts to disrupt NATO would displease the Americans and perhaps call the whole enterprise into question. Article 113 established a Common Commercial Policy, which empowered the Commission to negotiate trade agreements with third countries under a mandate from the Council. Inevitably these had wider political connotations, but the initial position was that the European Economic Community should concern itself exclusively with trade and not foreign affairs. Indeed during the Gaullist period the Community institutions went to considerable lengths to disavow any intention of trespassing on national preserves, and the Commission was rigorously excluded from involvement in foreign affairs other than where trade was concerned. It did maintain a low-level presence at the United Nations in New York to represent the Community interest on trade policy questions and this allowed for some informal co-ordination between the national delegations, but major political issues were dealt with bilaterally by the ambassadors.

However following the period of consolidation in the sixties the advantages of the member states acting together in the foreign policy field became increasingly apparent, particularly in those areas where commercial policy and foreign affairs overlapped. Moreover the mere existence of the Community with its structure of councils and subordinate bodies engendered the habit of co-operation between governments and this applied naturally to external issues. The Hague Summit of 1969 requested the Foreign Ministers of the Six to chart the objectives and methods of systematic foreign policy co-operation and the results of their work were published as the Luxembourg Report in 1970. This established European Political Co-operation (EPC), based on regular meetings of foreign ministers, outside the framework of the Treaties, to examine issues of common concern and co-ordinate foreign policy where there was a common interest in so doing.[1] EPC operated by consensus; there was no voting and the presidency of the Council was responsible for convening meetings and issuing policy declarations embodying the consensus reached. The Foreign Ministers meeting in Political Co-operation were supported by the so-called Davignon Committee, composed of the political directors of the different Foreign Affairs ministries; their job was to prepare meetings and reach preliminary agreements rather along the lines of COREPER. Following British accession and the establishment of the European Council, the Copenhagen Report of 1973 provided that the summit meetings should pay particular attention to external affairs and review the member states' relations in different parts of the world where there was a common interest. Working groups of junior officials were established on an ad hoc basis to look at specific geographic and functional areas. The report by Leo Tindemans, then Prime Minister of Belgium, on the future development of the European Union placed a heavy emphasis on the importance of speaking with one voice on foreign policy issues.

EPC enjoyed a considerable success during the CSCE negotiations which culminated in the signing of the Helsinki Final Act in 1975. It is ironic that the Conference on European Security which the Soviets had sought for a number of years as a means of dividing Europeans among themselves and driving a wedge between them and their American allies should have resulted in a significant strengthening of Western solidarity. Although the member states were separately represented the Presidency, supported by a team of Commission officials, was given responsibility for putting forward a collective point of view. As a result the EC countries secured important concessions in Basket 2, Economic Co-operation and Basket 3, Human Rights, the implementation of which was monitored in a series of follow-up conferences. At these the Presidency was given the power to adopt CSCE declarations on behalf of the Community as a whole.

The Foreign Ministers produced a number of Declarations

during the seventies, the most significant of which concerned the Middle East in the aftermath of the Yom Kippur War; European interests were seen to go rather further than the uncritical support for Israel which characterized the United States. The Venice Declaration of June 1980 represented a substantial breakthrough, recognizing as it did the special position of Palestine and the right of her people to a measure of self-determination. This was significantly different to the position of the USA and was widely believed to mark the beginning of a nascent common European foreign policy.

Britain had always been expected to draw on her experience as a permanent member of the UN Security Council and her remaining world-wide interests and take the lead in developing a stronger role for the Community in foreign affairs. While in opposition, Margaret Thatcher had criticized the Europeans for failing to capitalize on their economic strength to influence the course of world affairs. In a speech in Brussels in June 1978 entitled 'The Sinews of Foreign Policy' she said:

> We need far better machinery for ensuring that Community decisions in matters of trade and finance are in harmony with our European political interests, for example as they affect Turkey, Yugoslavia, Australia and New Zealand.
>
> To us in Europe these Community decisions may seem detailed economic matters about levies, tariffs and quotas, to be settled as best we can to suit the interests of European producers. But these decisions affect, often substantially, the ability of some of our friends overseas to continue as our friends. We have created an instrument but have not yet learned to use it in our own vital interests.
>
> The Commission and the Council of Ministers need to be more farsighted, more political in their approach. The Soviet Union would not dream of taking such decisions on technical grounds only.[2]

She went on to make a strong case for the Community being 'More than just an economic and cultural entity', but a spiritual force based on Christian beliefs in the essential dignity of man and his right to decide his own destiny along with liberty, responsibility, duty and justice. In 1975 Mrs Thatcher had taken the lead in establishing the European Democratic Union

(EDU), a grouping of Conservative and Christian Democrat Parties which was intended to counterbalance increasing co-operation between European Socialists. The principle achievement of the British Presidency of 1981 was the London Report which established a secretariat for EPC, based in Brussels, and staffed by diplomats seconded by national governments for the purpose. Until that time this role had been played by the Presidency itself, a burden which some of the smaller member states found impossible to fulfil.[3] The London Report also cautiously extended EPC to cover the 'economic aspects of security policy'.

The Soviet invasion of Afghanistan in December 1979 revealed the impotence of the Community in reacting speedily to outside events: the member states were unable to agree on a limited number of economic sanctions until 1982. Once such decisions were taken it was well equipped to implement agreed measures, for example the trade sanctions against the revolutionary Islamic regime in Iran, and later the economic blockade of Argentina during the Falklands War, but such action appeared ad hoc rather than part of the coherent and principled policy that Margaret Thatcher had advocated. In November 1981 the foreign ministers of Germany and Italy, Hans-Dietrich Genscher and Emilio Colombo launched a joint initiative which came to be known as the Draft European Act. This envisaged a much more intensive political co-operation, supervised by the European Council and with the active involvement of the European Parliament. In his speech to the Parliament presenting the document Mr Genscher said, 'We know we must proceed with caution . . . but we believe it is absolutely essential for the political and economic aspects of European security to be brought within the common foreign policy of the future.'[4]

The initiative was greeted with guarded enthusiasm, but soon ran out of steam; the concept of a European political union which became so important as to justify a separate inter-governmental conference ten years later, was too bold for the majority of the member states in 1981. The Draft European Act and a parallel memorandum from the new French Government of François Mitterrand which barely mentioned foreign policy, were examined by the foreign ministers and much of its language was reproduced in the Solemn Declaration on

European Union adopted at Stuttgart in June 1983. In the list of Community objectives the heads of government undertook to:

> Strengthen and develop European Political Co-operation through the elaboration and adoption of joint positions and joint action, on the basis of intensified consultations in the area of foreign policy including the co-ordination of the positions of member states on the political and economic aspects of security, so as to promote and facilitate the progressive development of such decisions and actions in a growing number of foreign policy fields.

Although the Stuttgart Declaration was hailed as a significant redefinition of the Community's goals – Chancellor Kohl described it as 'A step in the right direction at the right time' – it was too imprecise to be more than a wish list. Mrs Thatcher regarded it as a collection of grandiloquent phrases with little practical content. As so often happened she failed to see that apparently meaningless verbiage often concealed commitments to move forward which would be picked up and developed later to the discomfort of those who had signed up to them confident that the others would 'never get their act together'. It should come as no surprise that much of the language of the Stuttgart Declaration reappeared in more concrete form in the Single European Act.

Back in 1975 the foreign ministers had agreed to answer both written and oral questions from the European Parliament and this was supplemented by occasional debates on issues with which EPC had been concerned. The foreign ministers made an annual report to the Parliament on progress within EPC and a system of quarterly *colloques* involving the Presidency and the EP's Political Affairs Committee was instituted at which the parliamentarians were briefed confidentially on issues that were being discussed in the EPC framework. Direct elections produced a significant increase in Parliamentary interest, the number of questions asked rose rapidly and the occasional debates became more acrimonious. However as often as not the Presidency failed to take part in Parliamentary debates on foreign policy, which consequently lost much of their point. Under pressure, the answers to questions which were prepared by a group of junior officials from the representations became increasingly anodyne, the standard answer being either that the matter had not been discussed or that there was no consensus to report. Unsurprisingly Spinelli's draft treaty adopted by the European Parliament in 1984 called for Foreign Affairs to become a competence of the Union, with the Commission making proposals for common decision by Council and Parliament.

While there was no question of going as far as that there was a general recognition that EPC was an inadequate instrument for the EC's ambitions to influence world affairs. The 1985 Intergovernmental Conference (IGC) considered a number of suggestions for improving the working of EPC and their conclusions formed an important element of the Single European Act (SEA) which was signed in February 1986. The preamble contained the following *considerants*:

> Aware of the responsibility incumbent upon Europe to aim at speaking ever increasingly with one voice and to act with consistency and solidarity in order more effectively to protect its common interests and independence, in particular to display the principles of democracy and compliance with the law and of human rights to which they are attached.
> So that together they may make their own contribution to the preservation of peace and security in accordance with the undertaking entered into by them within the framework of the United Nations Charter.

Title III concerned itself with 'European Co-operation in the sphere of foreign policy', and the provisions are set out in Article 30. The member states bound themselves to inform and consult each other in advance on any foreign policy matter of general interest, and take the positions of their partners into account before adopting final positions of their own. Common principles and objectives were to be developed as a basis for common action, and nothing would be done to impair the ability of the Community to act as a cohesive force or block the formation of a consensus.

The Ministers for Foreign Affairs could discuss EPC questions at regular meetings of the Council, thus ending the distinction between EPC and the Council proper. For the first time the Commission was directly associated with Political

Co-operation, with the right to be present at EPC meetings and, along with the Presidency, was given the responsibility of ensuring that policy making was consistent. The role of the European Parliament was recognized with an undertaking that its views would be duly taken into consideration.

As regards mechanics, Paragraph 6 provided for close co-ordination on the political and economic aspects of security and Paragraph 7 required Member States to work together in international bodies so that EPC positions should be properly reflected in those international organizations where not all members were represented.[5] The Presidency was given the responsibility for 'initiating action and coordinating and representing the positions of Member States', supported by the Committee of Political Directors, which in common with the Ministers themselves, could be convened within 48 hours, if three member states requested. A new European Correspondents Group, responsible for monitoring the implementation of EPC decisions, and a permanent EPC Secretariat were based in Brussels. These arrangements which were given a treaty base for the first time were fleshed out in an accompanying declaration dealing with relations with the European Parliament, co-operation between overseas missions and the responsibilities of the Secretariat. Significantly the whole Title was to be reviewed in five years to see if further revisions were necessary.

The 1985 IGC and the SEA were dominated by economic issues, notably the Single Market, but the importance of Title III should not be underestimated. For the first time foreign policy making was anchored securely within the structure of the Treaties, and though EPC remained outside the jurisdiction of the Court of Justice, it was clearly a Community competence. Moreover the commitment to a review within a specified period ensured that this was a step on the road to the fully fledged Common Foreign and Security Policy envisaged by the Stuttgart Declaration and not an end in itself. For the first time the European Community had the mechanisms available to enable the necessary consensus to be speedily established so that it would have the ability to react decisively to international events.

The immediate result was a rapid increase in the number of Declarations issued by the Foreign Ministers, covering the

Middle East, Latin America, the various wars in Africa, human rights and most significantly the Soviet Union. There were signs that Gorbachev's new liberalism, characterized by the twin doctrines of glasnost and perestroika, was producing a thaw in relations with the Community, which had never been officially recognized by the USSR; the process was given a massive boost with the announcement in 1987 that the Soviet forces would be withdrawn from Afghanistan. Gorbachev's speeches in which he referred to our 'Common European House' had struck a chord particularly in Germany where there had been widespread opposition to the deployment of Cruise and Pershing missiles, but these benevolent signals had to be set against the continuing suppression of nationalist movements in the Baltic States. Out of the blue a Treaty on Intermediate Nuclear Forces (INF) was agreed bilaterally by Presidents Reagan and Gorbachev in the Autumn of 1988, underlining that the tectonic plates of the post-war settlement were beginning to shift at last. More than ever the lack of a coherent mechanism to express a distinctive European approach to the geopolitical problems of the day was apparent; declarations however well intended were simply not sufficient.

These weaknesses were embarrassingly exposed by the dramatic series of revolutionary events in Eastern Europe, culminating in the collapse of the USSR at the end of 1991. The European Community watched in awe as one by one the Communist regimes of Central and Eastern Europe crumbled; in each case the new non-Communist government affirmed its attachment to the principles of private ownership, free competition and open markets, and announced that joining the European Community was their most important political goal. Amid heady talk of a 'New World Order' and a new security structure for Europe guaranteed by the CSCE, it seemed that everything that the Founding Fathers had prophesied was about to become true; the 'Ever Closer Union' was about to be sanctified by the most remarkable political success. It soon became clear however that shaking off the dead hand of Communism was not in itself a guarantee of stability and rising living standards. The transition from a command economy to a free market involved huge adjustments, and it was by no means clear that the populations in the newly liberalized states who had been led to believe that capitalism was a passport to instant prosperity, would be prepared to endure the pain that the transition involved. Jobs for life and guaranteed wages disappeared at a stroke and the purchasing power of local currencies plummeted. While shop windows quickly filled with shiny Western consumer goods, few could afford to buy them and a feeling of disillusion rapidly set in.

The European Community was encouraged by the Americans to take the lead in the Group of 24 States which came together to co-ordinate aid to the newly liberalized countries and itself provided more than 40 per cent of the funds. Central and Eastern Europe was tacitly accepted as a European sphere of influence. The Commission drawing on its experience with Association Agreements and the indicative aid programmes drawn up in the framework of the Lomé Conventions, put together two programmes: PHARE for Poland, Hungary, Czechoslovakia, and later Bulgaria, Romania and Albania; and TACIS for those parts of the former Soviet Union that were now independent republics within the Commonwealth of Independent States. Following a French initiative the European Bank for Reconstruction and Development (EBRD) was established to channel investment to the newly liberalized countries and promote the development of infrastructure and private industry.

In spite of the good intentions which lay behind these initiatives it soon became clear that they were quite inadequate to deal with the scale of the challenge. It was not so much lack of funds, though this was inevitably a factor, but more a failure to understand the nature of the problem and recognize that conventional economic assistance programmes designed for developing countries of the Third World were inappropriate to the needs of Central and Eastern European countries which were already industrialized, but starved of investment and modern technology.[6] Much of the money was spent on consultancy and identifying projects for further spending; much went straight into the pockets of new 'entrepreneurs'. The Commission lacked the manpower and experience to monitor its contractual agents; there was no overarching concept as had been the case with Marshall Aid, or targets against which progress could measured. The EBRD, which under its first President, Jacques Attali, a confidant of President Mitterrand, spent more on embellishing its building and setting up its administration than it actually advanced in loans and this became a symbol of the Community's failure to live up to expectations.

Despite the rhetoric there was a marked reluctance among some member states to adopt the kind of market opening measures that would have done more than anything else to revive the traumatized economies of Eastern and Central Europe. Throwing money at the problem in the form of official aid seemed preferable to adding to competitive pressures at a time when Western Europe was sliding into recession. As a result the Europe Agreements which were designed to establish new trading relationships proved extremely difficult to negotiate and in many cases fell well short of expectations. This produced a sense of disillusion among the people in the liberalizing countries which no doubt contributed to the return to power of many reformed Communists at successive elections;[7] free market liberals seemed to have been abandoned by their western patrons. Perhaps this merely serves to underline the truth that economic salvation lies in the hands of the people themselves and is not in the gift of benevolent outsiders.

The Community's attitude to the Central and Eastern European countries was bedevilled by ambivalence. Until the Copenhagen Summit of 1993 it was not universally accepted that they should ever become members of the EC itself: the idea of a exclusive Fortress Europe, composed of a core of wealthy countries held together by a Single Market and Single Currency, had much appeal for those member states which instinctively distrusted open trade. Once it became clear that the CSCE was incapable of guaranteeing security, questions were inevitably raised about relations with Russia and whether too much Western interference in the former satellites might provoke a hostile reaction. It was not clear whether the Central European countries were to be treated as partners on course for EC membership as soon as liberalization was consolidated and recovery assured, or as an economic and political buffer zone between the EC and the unstable giant to the east. As so often, the Community countries were prepared to endorse the objectives of stability, security and prosperity for all, but unprepared to furnish the means with anything like the clear-sightedness and political determination required.

The crisis triggered by the Iraqi occupation of Kuwait in August 1990 revealed further fault lines in EPC. The

Community initially reacted speedily and effectively by impos-
ing economic sanctions on Iraq but then quickly fell apart
over direct intervention. Some countries such as Britain and
France endorsed the United Nations approach and contributed troops to the expeditionary force. By contrast Germany,
preoccupied by events in Eastern Europe and the increasing
pacifism of its population, sheltered behind constitutional constraints on the deployment of forces outside the NATO area,
whereas some smaller countries such as Ireland and Denmark
refused to have anything to do with military action. Once the
economic sanctions, which were clearly within the sphere of
Community competence, were successfully initiated by the Commission, each member state pursued its own course of action
with little sign of internal consistency or coherence. As a result the United States was left with the responsibility of pro-
secuting the war to a successful conclusion and deciding when
the fighting should stop. In spite of the pretensions of the
Europeans and their long-standing interests in the Middle East,
which is geographically in their back yard, they had little dis-
cernible influence on the course of events.

These experiences, coupled with the unification of Germany,
which has been dealt with in Chapter 7, reignited the demand
for political union to be delivered by the second intergovernmental conference. The term Political Union has been interpreted in Britain as meaning the assimilation of sovereign
nations in an all embracing federal superstate, but this is a
caricature. In fact political union was driven by the desire of
Chancellor Kohl to anchor the newly united Germany firmly
in the democratic camp by strengthening the common institutions, and a sense that Europe needed a common and consistent foreign policy if she was to protect her vital interests. In
both cases the perception was that the will was there but the
mechanisms were missing. Much of the negotiation in the IGC
focused on the mechanisms, the key questions being whether
CFSP should remain intergovernmental or be brought within
the conventional institutional structure and to what extent policy and action should be determined by majority voting.

The text that finally emerged in Title V of the Treaty of European Union represented a significant victory for the intergov-
ernmentalists. CFSP remained detached from the European
Community proper as a new pillar of the European Union,

and as such it is outside the jurisdiction of the Court of Justice. The Commission is fully associated with CFSP, but has no special status and the European Parliament is merely given the right to be informed and to ask questions, the provisions covering the Commission and Parliament simply reproduce the language of the SEA.

The objectives of CFSP in Article J.1 were limited to generalities:

— to safeguard the common values, fundamental interests and independence of the Union;
— to strengthen the security of the Union and its member states in all ways;
— to preserve peace and strengthen international security, in accordance with the principles of the United Nations Charter as well as the principles of the Helsinki Final Act and the objectives of the Paris Charter;
— to promote international co-operation;
— to develop and consolidate democracy and the rule of law, and respect for human rights and fundamental freedoms.

These objectives are to be achieved through systematic co-operation along the lines determined in the SEA and through joint action. The Treaty also lays down that:

The Member States shall support the Union's external and security policy actively and unreservedly in a spirit of loyalty and mutual solidarity. They shall refrain from any action which is contrary to the interests of the Union or likely to impair its effectiveness as a cohesive force in international relations. The Council shall ensure that these principles are complied with. (Article J.1(4))

Article J.2 provides for consultation and co-operation in the pursuit of common positions, again drawing on the language of the SEA. Article J.3 introduces a new concept of joint action. The Council is given the responsibility for deciding in principle on joint action, according to general guidelines laid down by the European Council, and agreeing on the means to be employed to achieve it. This includes defining those issues which are to be decided by a qualified majority vote.[8]

Once joint action is decided member states are committed

to support it and consult with the Council before any national action is taken in the context of joint action other than the simple implementation of Council decisions. Article J.3(7) states:

> Should there be any major difficulties in implementing a joint action, a Member State shall refer them to the Council which shall discuss them and seek solutions. Such solutions shall not run counter to the objectives of the joint action or impair its effectiveness.

In other words once a joint action is decided upon member states who disagree with it or the way in which it is implemented must remain passive. Any member state or the Commission may raise a CFSP issue in the Council and the Presidency has the ability on request to convene a meeting of the Council within 48 hours or even faster if circumstances warrant. The Committee of Political Directors established by the SEA is strengthened with the ability to deliver opinions to the Council and Article J.11(2) allows the Council to decide whether operational expenditure should be charged to the EC Budget or to individual member states.

As far as the CFSP is concerned the Maastricht provisions produce a hybrid. Although the intentions are explicit the process can only be activated if there is unanimity among the member states and majority voting only becomes possible if all the members agree. This provides an effective answer to those who suggested that Maastricht involved a substantial surrender of independence as regards foreign affairs; each member state retains an effective veto over common action being launched – only consultation and co-operation are mandatory, but there is no provision for enforcement or judicial review. The suggestion that Britain would not have been permitted to mount the operation to recover the Falklands if the CFSP had been in force is demonstrably wrong.

The relative ineffectiveness of CFSP is illustrated by the guidelines that the European Council issued as a basis for joint action at the meeting in October 1993 to mark the coming into force of the Treaty on European Union. These were:

> Promotion of peace and stability in Europe.
> Support for the Middle East peace process.

Support for transition to multiracial democracy in South Africa.

Search for a negotiated and durable solution to the conflict in former Yugoslavia.

These were the product of a report by the Foreign Ministers to the Lisbon Council in the June of the previous year and gave rise to joint actions covering humanitarian convoys in Bosnia and the designation of priority routes, sending a team of observers to the Russian elections, establishing a framework of co-operation for the transition of South Africa to majority rule and instituting an embargo on Libya. In none of these were the majority voting procedures applied and in no case was there any obvious source of controversy. As the House of Commons Select Committee on Foreign Affairs pointed out:

> It appears that a common foreign policy may not, in the immediate future look very different from European Polit-ical Co-operation as practised by the Community in recent years. Co-operation as practised by the Community has been getting closer for some time.[9]

The crisis in former Yugoslavia which broke out in June 1991 when the IGC was in full swing produced an early test of the efficacy of CFSP which nearly proved fatal. When the crisis broke, with declarations of independence by Slovenia and Croatia in June 1991, many in the Community saw it as an opportunity to atone for shortcomings over the Gulf, especi-ally when the troika of foreign ministers undertook a mission immediately following the Luxembourg European Council and seemed to be making progress. 'This shows what the Com-munity can achieve if it works together on foreign policy', announced President Delors when these early efforts at medi-ation showed signs of success.[10] The subsequent deployment of white-uniformed Community peace monitors seemed to have brought a rapid end to the fighting in Slovenia, though in fact the Yugoslav National Army showed no stomach for a long fight in the Slovene mountains. The President in Office of the Council, Jacques Poos of Luxembourg, was heard to observe: 'This is the hour of Europe, not the hour of the Americans.'[11] Such complacency merely exacerbated the initial misjudgement that the Yugoslav Federation could be preserved and ensured that no collective action was taken to stop the escalation of the real conflict until it was far too late.

The Community's original mistake was to overestimate the capacity for survival of the Yugoslav Federation; ever since Tito's death the strains between the ethnic minorities within the various republics had threatened to blow it apart, but the EC remained convinced that support for the Federal Government was the best way of averting a crisis. The Milan Council of October 1990 had called specifically for 'the preservation of the unity and territorial integrity of Yugoslavia'. The Commission in particular was keen to do everything possible to defend the Federation, the Yugoslav Joint Association Agreement had operated successfully for a number of years, officials at all levels were accustomed to dealing with their Yugoslav opposite numbers and in many cases had formed close friendships. Prime Minister Markovic was a regular visitor to Brussels, and preserving the Federation under his leadership seemed infinitely preferable to accepting the separatist ambitions of Presidents Milosevic and Tudjman. Following the apparently successful Brioni accords, brokered by the Community in July, it seemed that this might be achieved, but as the conflict between Serbia and Croatia intensified, the divisions between the member states themselves became increasingly exposed.

By the beginning of October it was clear that the Federation was doomed. Germany, which had strong cultural and ethnic links with Slovenia and Croatia and bitter memories of fighting with Serb partisans during the war, was increasingly anxious to recognize the breakaway states. Natural sympathy for the Croats was combined with a fear of mass migration if their demands for independence were not granted. After a furious row at the foreign ministers' meeting on 16 December, criteria for the recognition of the Yugoslav republics were drawn up and a Commission under Robert Badinter appointed to report which of them complied. On this basis the Germans agreed to delay recognition for a month. The Badinter report was duly produced and suggested that Croatia did not meet the required criteria; nonetheless German determination prevailed and in the name of Community solidarity all the member states recognized Slovenia and Croatia on 16 January 1992. It was, according to Piet Dankert, the Dutch Secretary of State for Foreign

Affairs, 'a very unhappy beginning' for closer co-operation on foreign and security policy.[12]

It is particularly ironic that the Kohl Government should have been largely responsible for the disarray of Community policy towards the Yugoslav republics. Throughout the build-up to Maastricht, the German Chancellor had been the foremost proponent of a political union characterized by majority voting, on the grounds that this would be the best way of ensuring that Germany would not be tempted to seek some kind of hegemony over the rest of Europe. There seems little doubt that had a vote been taken at the 16 December Council it would have opposed early recognition of the republics, but Germany, within days of signing the Treaty of European Union, was prepared to override the consensus of her partners by threatening unilateral action.

Recognition set off a chain reaction; the Bosnian Government organized a referendum on independence which was boycotted by the Serb minority and so produced an overwhelming vote for secession, the Community had no choice but to recognize the Republic of Bosnia which was immediately confronted by a Serb uprising. Macedonia, which had fulfilled the Badinter criteria, declared herself independent, but recognition was blocked by Greece who claimed that an independent Republic of Macedonia threatened her territorial integrity. The Lisbon Council failed to resolve the situation and merely took note of the Greek objection; once again it had been shown that a member state determined to protect its national interest could paralyse the Community whatever the apparent commitment to a CFSP.

The Yugoslav crisis dealt a savage blow to the European Union's ambitions to play a significant role in world affairs. Their official mediator Lord Carrington negotiated a succession of cease-fire agreements which were routinely broken before the ink on the paper was dry. The Community had no means of enforcing the deals it had brokered and its peace monitors were reduced to observing an increasingly vicious conflict. The destruction of Vukovar knocked Croatia out of the war and the Bosnian Serbs were able to take over large amounts of territory and lay siege to Sarajevo. It was clear that the Union was incapable of resolving the crisis on its own and the London Conference of August 1992 launched a joint EU-UN peace initiative which in its turn was to run into the buffers of ethnic intransigence. Primacy on the ground passed to the United Nations, which deployed troops to protect relief convoys and carry out peacekeeping operations and the diplomatic effort became the province of the Contact Group of America, Russia, Britain, France and Germany. The EU's official mediator, by now Lord Owen, seemed an increasingly isolated and futile figure.

The Yugoslav crisis has shown that the EU member states are able to sustain a common position in that they have remained united in their objectives. Unlike the Balkan wars at the beginning of the century there has been no suggestion of different European powers seeking to achieve their national goals by playing the different protagonists off against each other. To that extent the member states have remained united and helped prevent the conflict from spreading. However as Germany and Greece have demonstrated in their different ways solidarity can easily become an end in itself, so that the CFSP becomes a hostage to an individual partner determined to pursue a particular interest. It also shows that mediation which is not backed by the threat of force will only succeed if the parties to the dispute are themselves minded to settle their differences.

The contrast with the Gulf is instructive; America was prepared to deploy troops and fight if necessary, Iraq was compelled to leave Kuwait as a result. The EU countries were never prepared to deploy troops to enforce a peace settlement in Yugoslavia and their mediation efforts were ignored despite economic sanctions. No amount of common policies and diplomatic mechanisms will work unless the political determination to enforce the collective will is present and this in turn depends on the ability to mobilize public opinion in support of the common objectives. For all the posturing in the summer of 1991, public opinion in the EC was not prepared to endorse the deployment of troops in sufficient numbers to resolve the crisis nor was there any sign that people in general believed that common action by the Community could provide a solution. On the contrary, opinion in Germany and Greece was a powerful factor in influencing the governments to pursue an independent line. Europe will not succeed in fulfilling her ambitions to play a part on the world stage unless her own citizens believe that this is the way forward for them and are prepared to commit themselves wholehcartedly to the common cause.

The Yugoslav experience also teaches us that no single power, with the possible exception of the United States, is in a position to take unilateral action to resolve a conflict or protect its vital interests. Not one of the partners was in a position to pursue an independent policy on Yugoslavia and such success as there has been came from their acting together. An effective CFSP is essential if the European partners are to protect their vital interests effectively. The Yugoslav experience shows how much further they have to go before they are in a position to do so. No amount of common policies and diplomatic mechanisms can substitute for political determination to define and carry through the collective will with the full-hearted support of public opinion. This in turn requires self-confident and clear-sighted leadership, qualities that have been so far in short supply where the CFSP is concerned.

9 Defence and Security: A new world order

One of the driving forces which led to the establishment of the European Coal and Steel Community (ECSC) in 1950 was Robert Schuman's perception that the best way of preventing war between France and Germany in the future was to pool production of the main manufacturing inputs so neither country would be able to run a separate armaments industry. At that time the Cold War was at its most intense, Europe was divided between the Communist East and the free West, and in spite of the lifting of the Berlin blockade there was a continuing fear of the military threat from the Soviet Union. Monnet and Schuman had based their plans for a union of European states on a European Defence Community (EDC), on the grounds that this was the area in which co-operation was most urgent and necessary. It was only when EDC was killed by British indifference and a negative vote in the French National Assembly, that the attention of the Founding Fathers turned to economic co-operation as the best route to a united Europe, and the Messina Conference was convened to begin negotiations to set up what became the European Economic Community (EEC). Common defence has always been a factor in the European debate, and an important goal for European federalism, but because of the trauma over EDC it was placed in cold storage; for over thirty years defence was the exclusive province of the Atlantic Alliance.

The Brussels Treaty of 1948 was a direct response to the Soviet threat to Berlin and brought Britain, France and the Benelux countries together in a defensive alliance, based on the 1947 Dunkirk Treaty between France and the UK. Article 5 contained an explicit commitment on the part of the signatories to come to the assistance of any one of them that was attacked. The same terminology in slightly weaker form was used in Article 5 of the Washington Treaty of 1949 which linked the Brussels partners with America and Canada in the North Atlantic Treaty Organization (NATO), along with Denmark, Norway, Greece, Turkey and Iceland. NATO provided the vehicle for a continuing American commitment to the defence of Europe and the basis for the deployment of American troops in Germany as the Occupation came to an end. The defence commitments contained in the Brussels Treaty were assigned to the new organization, and following the collapse of EDC in 1953, the British Foreign Secretary, Sir Anthony Eden, proposed that Germany and Italy be added to the signatories as new members of the organization that was renamed Western European Union (WEU). The Treaty was modified to reflect its relationship with NATO and two new institutions, a Arms Control Agency and a Parliamentary Assembly composed of delegates to the Council of Europe were set up. In 1955 a Standing Armaments Committee was established with the object of improving co-operation in arms procurement, this subsequently became known as Euro-Group.

The WEU continued in being but was overshadowed by NATO; the Ministerial Council met occasionally and made an annual report to the Parliamentary Assembly; the WEU Secretariat was based in London and a research institute was maintained in Paris. Meanwhile the European Community was excluded from all aspects of defence and security, Article 223 of the Treaty of Rome had the effect of exempting defence products from the normal rules of the Common Market, facilitating the retention of independent national arms industries.[1]

The tensions of the Cold War era gradually became easier and the Helsinki Conference, which concluded in 1975, ushered in a period of detente with the Soviet bloc. As the perception of an armed threat from the Soviet Union weakened, peace movements gained in strength and the deployment of American nuclear weapons on European soil was increasingly questioned. The Germans were especially conscious that their country would be the primary battlefield if a nuclear war did break out and felt great bitterness at the thought that flexible response in practice would mean the Germans taking all the casualties. In 1978 NATO, in response to the Soviet deployment of SS-20 intermediate range missiles targeted at Western Europe, adopted the two-track decision which involved continuing detente but at the same time deploying its own intermediate range missiles to counterbalance the Soviet threat. The deployment of cruise and Pershing missiles proved extremely unpopular with European public opinion and there were mass demonstrations, sometimes degenerating into riots, in all countries but particularly in Germany. The NATO Council stuck to its guns and the missiles were successfully deployed, but at the cost of considerable damage to the Alliance's image and the unquestioning acceptance of American leadership. It became clear that public support for collective defence could not be maintained if Europeans saw themselves as cannon fodder for the US military machine; accordingly the question of an independent European defence identity began to move up the agenda. The Genscher-Colombo Draft European Act made reference to 'coordination of security policy . . . in order to safeguard Europe's independence, protect its vital interests and strengthen its security'; the Stuttgart Declaration was more circumspect, referring simply to 'the coordination of positions of Member States on the political and economic aspects of security in the Section on Foreign Policy'. The word defence was nowhere mentioned.

No doubt such considerations were uppermost in the minds of WEU Defence Ministers when in 1984 they met in Rome to celebrate the 30th Anniversary of the signing of the Brussels Treaty and decided to reactivate the organization. They announced that the WEU Council of Foreign and Defence Ministers should meet twice yearly, that the Presidency should revolve on an annual basis and there would be improved contacts with the Parliamentary Assembly and with the non-WEU members of NATO.

As we have seen, Title III of the 1987 Single European Act (SEA) provided a treaty basis for European political cooperation; in addition it incorporated the Stuttgart language on security:

> The High Contracting Parties consider that closer cooperation on questions of European security would contribute in an essential way to the development of a European identity in external policy matters. They are ready to coordinate their positions more closely on the political and economic aspects of security.

and at the insistence of Britain it went on to add:

> Nothing in this Title shall impede closer co-operation between certain of the High Contracting Parties within the

framework of the Western European Union or the Atlantic Alliance.[2]

The point was that the positions of the individual member states was too contradictory for a satisfactory defence policy to be evolved. Ireland as a neutral felt compelled to block any discussion of defence which might be contrary to her constitution; Denmark was a loyal member of NATO but wholly opposed to any European involvement in the defence and security field; France had quit NATO's integrated command structure in 1960 and was keen on the construction of a European defence pillar; Germany was a loyal member of the Alliance but saw such a pillar as a way round constitutional limits on the activities of her defence forces; Britain felt strongly that any flirtation with a separate European defence structure risked alienating the Americans and destabilizing NATO. The IGC clearly concluded that for the time being defence was better left to the WEU, though the undertaking to review Title III after five years meant that it remained on the agenda.

These conclusions were followed up by the WEU Council. The conclusions of a Council meeting in Luxembourg in 1987 pointed out that WEU could play a significant role in the development of a European Union and drew attention to the importance of strengthening the European component of the NATO Alliance. In October the same year, ministers adopted the Hague Platform which was intended to provide the basis for the WEU's further development. The second paragraph of the preamble made a clear link between European Union and defence in a way that had not been possible since the days of EDC.

> We recall our commitment to build a European Union in accordance with the Single European Act which we all signed as Members of the European Community. We are convinced that the construction of an integrated Europe will remain incomplete as long as it does not include security and defence.

The Hague document also made a specific reference to NATO's nuclear deterrent as an essential component of European defence.

The meeting of Presidents Reagan and Gorbachev at Reykjavik in the autumn of 1988 marked a significant turning-point in relations between the superpowers. Its significance lay in the fact that the Americans and the Russians concluded a bilateral deal without any reference to their allies, underlining the fact that their own national interests took priority in disarmament negotiations. The immediate consequence was the Treaty on Intermediate Nuclear Forces (INF) which committed its signatories to the removal and destruction of a whole class of medium range missiles including SS-20s, cruise and Pershings, something that had never been possible before and a complete vindication of NATO's twin-track strategy. However it raised serious questions about the future of collective defence. The removal of intermediate range missiles made a nuclear attack less likely, and it was possible that public opinion would demand the removal of all nuclear forces notwithstanding the Soviets' overwhelming superiority in conventional forces. Should these be mobilized to attack NATO, there were obvious doubts as to whether an American president would be prepared to put his own cities at risk by using his intercontinental missiles as a deterrent.

The Germans demanded that tactical nuclear weapons such as the French Pluton also be removed, as their limited range meant they could only fall on East or West Germany. President Mitterrand countered by proposing the formation of a joint Franco-German Brigade, containing troops from both armies, to be stationed in Germany within reach of these short range missiles. Meanwhile Margaret Thatcher was arguing for a strengthening of the tactical deterrent in the shape of stand-off missiles launched from the air (TASMS), and submarine-launched cruise missiles (SLCMS) which were compatible with the INF Treaty and plugged the gap between ICBMs and conventional forces. It was evident that after Reykjavik a major rethink of Allied strategy was essential.

The debate in Europe was echoed in America where President Gorbachev's personal charm had made a great impression. Indeed there were those who argued that the Americans and Russians could achieve a bilateral accord which could be imposed on Europe if necessary; as American diplomats were wont to point out, the USA and the USSR historically had a great deal in common: the main source of tension between them was their intimate but ambivalent relationship with Europe. US public opinion found it hard to understand why it was necessary to keep large and expensive American forces stationed abroad at a time when the US Budget deficit was ballooning out of control. The WEU had successfully organized joint naval patrols in the Gulf, and for many Europeans its further development into a separate defence pillar was increasingly desirable. Others, particularly in Britain, recognizing that American logistical and weapons support was essential to the viability of NATO, were concerned that any development of WEU which excluded the Americans and Canadians would undermine their commitment to European defence and lead to the break-up of the Alliance. The Americans themselves were in two minds, on the one hand they were anxious to reduce their stationed forces and were constantly urging their allies to bear a greater share of the defence burden, at the same time American dominance of the Alliance was a prized asset which might be put at risk if there was too much European independence. The prospect that the European partners might come up with positions that they had agreed in advance and which could be presented to the Americans as *faits accomplis* which could not be subsequently unravelled, was particularly unwelcome. Within the Reagan and Bush administrations the State Department, particularly when James Baker was Secretary of State, favoured a more equal partnership, while the Department of Defense was determined to maintain US paramountcy within the Alliance. They found a doughty ally in the British Government, which until 1990 was rigidly opposed to any WEU pretensions; particularly in Conservative circles Americans were regarded as reliable allies and friends, in contrast with recent memories of perceived Continental pusillanimity at the time of the Falklands War. The NATO structure had proved itself over the years and there was a deepseated reluctance on the part of the military to change something that manifestly worked, for the uncertainties of a separate European pillar.

On the other side the semi-detached position of the French added to the uncertainties. De Gaulle had removed France from the command structure of NATO, insisting that her forces could not be under the control of an American supreme commander. As a result, although France remained committed to the Alliance and bound by the obligations of its Article 5, her forces were independent of the integrated command structure. Over the years the independence of the French forces and particularly of their nuclear deterrent had become a powerful symbol of French independence and no government would dare to propose reintegrating French forces into NATO. Indeed there were those in Paris who dreamed of breaking the transatlantic link in favour of a separate European defence system operating independently of Washington. This would have been wholly impracticable. The European forces were dependent on US logistical support to such an extent that they could not move troops to the battlefield without American transport; and even more to the point, the elaborate system of spy satellites and electronic communications known as SIGINT, was absolutely essential in providing the intelligence essential to fight a modern war and the European allies had neither the technology nor the budget to replace it. The Americans provided NATO forces with their eyes and ears as well as their legs, and the command structure reflected this dependence on American goodwill. The challenge therefore was to redefine NATO's objectives and maintain the Alliance's effectiveness, while accommodating America's desire to reduce sharply the numbers of US stationed forces.

The Franco-German brigade that Chancellor Kohl and President Mitterrand had established in 1987 as a symbol of their economic and political interdependence was a complicating factor. It gave substance to American and British fears that the Alliance was about to be broken up, while encouraging unrealistic French dreams of a separate European defence identity. Matters were not improved by the derision of the sturdier Atlanticists at the sight of two armies giving parade ground orders in different languages and the feeling that it was militarily unsound, characteristic of a willingness to subordinate defence realities to political symbolism. In the event it provided the Germans with a vehicle to draw the French closer to the Alliance by insisting that the Euro Corps, as the Brigade came to be known, be open to contingents of other European partners and be assigned to the WEU, thus creating a direct link to the NATO command itself. In that respect at least it did prove a model for future developments.

Meanwhile NATO, which in 1989 celebrated its fiftieth

anniversary, was also beginning to respond to the need for change. At a summit meeting in May that year the heads of government adopted a document entitled 'A Comprehensive Concept of Arms Control and Disarmament', which introduced a new doctrine of minimum deterrence:

> The basic goal of the Alliance's arms control policy is to enhance security and stability at the lowest balanced level of forces and armaments consistent with the requirements of the strategy of deterrence.

The declaration went on to call for the maintenance of a sub-strategic weapons capability, coupled with intensified negotiations for a balanced reduction of both conventional and nuclear forces.

The Alliance was thus compelled to rethink its strategy, particularly as regards the level of forces required in the new situation. The talks on the reduction of Conventional Forces in Europe (CFE) were the main theatre for negotiations between the two alliances; their objective was to achieve a rough balance in conventional forces, in which the Soviets had an overwhelming superiority, and establish adequate means for verifying that agreed reductions were carried out. In parallel there were bilateral talks between Russia and America to conclude a START treaty which would deal with strategic nuclear weapons.

This potentially dangerous atmosphere of uncertainty and disarray was largely resolved by the course of events. The collapse of the Warsaw Pact began with the revolutions in Poland in 1989 and proceeded rapidly through Hungary and Czechoslovakia. On 9 November the Berlin Wall was breached and the unification of the two Germanies moved to the head of the political agenda. This marked the decisive change in the military balance which had divided Europe since 1945; since Germany was to be one country again there could be no justification for the four-power status of Berlin and as the Russian forces were withdrawn there could clearly be wholesale reductions in the American presence.

At a North Atlantic Council meeting at Turnberry in June 1990 the Foreign Ministers called for a rapid conclusion to the CFE talks which would reduce Russian conventional forces in Europe to a point where they were incapable of launching a surprise attack or initiating large-scale offensive action. The status of Berlin was to be regularized by the so-called two plus four process, the two Germanies plus the four occupying powers, which would produce a treaty which would formally end the occupation established after the Second World War and the new security edifice would be crowned by a strengthened CSCE which would be responsible for maintaining security by consensus, promoting confidence-building measures and monitoring the implementation of arms agreements.

This was followed by the London Declaration of 6 July at which the heads of government redefined NATO's tasks as follows:

> NATO will field smaller and restructured active forces. These will be highly mobile and versatile so that the Allied leaders will have maximum flexibility in deciding how to respond to a crisis. It will rely increasingly on multi-national corps made up of national units.
> NATO will scale back the readiness of its active units, reducing training requirements and the number of exercises.
> NATO will rely more heavily on the ability to build up larger forces if and when they might be needed.

The Declaration went on to call for a follow-on treaty to CFE which would significantly reduce substrategic weapons and announced a strategic move away from forward defence and reduced reliance on nuclear weapons. The final phase of the process of disarmament was to be an enhanced CSCE foreshadowed at Turnberry with institutions capable of monitoring the agreements.

The Conference on Security and Co-operation in Europe (CSCE) which had been kept in being to monitor the Helsinki Agreement of 1975 had become a precursor for ending the Cold War and the parallel process of multilateral disarmament. CSCE offered the hope that disputes could be resolved by round table negotiations involving all European states, rather than bilaterally between two competing alliances. Deployment of intermediate range missiles in the early eighties had given rise to fears that Europe would simply become a battlefield for the nuclear superpowers and there was a strong body of opinion that yearned for a denuclearized Europe with the CSCE acting as a forum for consensus and peacekeeping. To such people Gorbachev's speeches in which he referred to 'Our Common European House' had great appeal, fuelling fears that public opinion would come to see the CSCE as an alternative to NATO. For idealists in the West a New World Order comprising all the democratic states in Europe sitting round the negotiating table on an equal basis and resolving disputes by agreement and peer group pressure rather than through military alliances and the threat of force was a beguiling prospect. The revolutions in Eastern Europe which led to the break-up of the Warsaw Pact seemed to justify this promise, especially as the governments of the newly liberalized countries were desperate to join some kind of international body which would underwrite their new-found independence. CSCE was particularly valuable in this respect as it brought together the US and Russia as well as the European countries. The Charter of Paris, signed in November 1990, reaffirmed the Helsinki principles and the commitment of the signatories to resolving disputes by peaceful means. It accepted the principle of common security and established permanent institutions in the shape of a Council of Ministers and a Committee of Senior Officials, which could be convened at short notice, serviced by a secretariat based in Prague. A Conflict Prevention Centre was set up in Vienna with a mission to promote exchange of information and co-operation between the national military establishments and develop confidence-building measures, and this would be supported by a Consultative Committee composed of Heads of Delegation to the disarmament negotiations. Finally an Office for Free Elections was set up in Warsaw with a remit to facilitate contacts and the exchange of information between participating states.

The hallmark of the CSCE process was consensus and this rapidly proved its undoing. Although missions were sent to seek solutions to the territorial disputes between Armenia and Azerbaijan over Nagorno-Karabakh, and between Georgia and her Caucasian neighbours, they achieved very little. More seriously when the civil war broke out in Yugoslavia, CSCE intervention was blocked by the Yugoslav Government itself which vetoed discussion of its internal affairs. Although the rules were amended subsequently to prevent the state concerned from having an effective veto, the damage had been done. The CSCE failed its most important test because none

of the members were prepared to concede the right to interference in the internal affairs of a member state without its
consent; with the end of the Cold War the tendency was for
conflicts to flare up between ethnic minorities within national
boundaries, seeking to give expression to aspirations which
had long been suppressed by the power politics of the previous era. Whereas the CSCE had provided a useful framework
for achieving the linked agreements which ended the Cold
War and formulating a set of principles to govern international
co-operation, the consensus rule made it completely impotent
in the face of domestic conflicts and thus irrelevant to the
needs of the time.

The WEU had gained some credibility through its co-
ordination of minesweeping operations in the Gulf in 1987,
and this was enhanced when Spain and Portugal joined its
ranks in 1988, the former after protracted negotiations to
accede to NATO. When Iraq seized Kuwait in August 1990, the
WEU Chiefs of Staff, including a number of Chiefs of Naval
Staff, met and established a military co-ordination group covering the operations of member states' naval forces assigned to
enforce the UN Security Council resolutions authorizing a
blockade of Iraq. This was subsequently extended to cover
land and air forces. At the height of the crisis WEU countries
had 30 warships deployed in the Gulf area and although each
was part of a separate national contingent, co-operation on
the ground in terms of both operations and logistics was very
close and seems to have worked well. This low-key success of
the WEU no doubt influenced the negotiators in the IGC.

Defence co-operation had been put on the table as a necessary element of political union, as President Delors put it in a
speech to the Institute of Strategic Studies in March 1991:

> The only option compatible with the complete vision of
> European Union is to insert a common security policy into
> this framework . . . We must make it clear that what we are
> proposing is a single community as a logical extension of
> the ambitions of European Union heralded by the Single
> European Act.[3]

The argument in the IGC was principally concerned with the
role of the neutral states such as Ireland and those like Denmark which had no wish to become members of WEU, and

whether defence should be anchored inside the Community structure as Delors advocated, or whether WEU should be the defence entity acting as a bridge between the EC and NATO. A British paper made it clear that defence and security should remain outside the framework of the Community treaties, but advocated dropping the limitation of Community interest to the political and economic aspects of security and bringing the WEU within the overall structure of the European Union. The British approach was summarized by Douglas Hurd in a newspaper article:

> Our approach to the Intergovernmental Conference is to say, 'Let us be European, but let us not be arrogant or unrealistic.' NATO must be an integral part of the future defence of Europe, it provides irreplaceable elements in our security not just for the time being but permanently. We need to work out in detail how the Alliance, the European input and the European Union will be linked.
>
> Interdependence not exclusivity is the key. An approach that emphasised the separateness of Europe would seriously weaken our real security.[4]

In the event it was the British gradualist approach that prevailed in the Treaty of European Union. Title V replaced Title III of the Single European Act and included a new Article, J4, on defence. The first two paragraphs read as follows:

1. The common foreign and security policy shall include all questions related to the security of the Union, including the eventual framing of a common defence policy, which might in time lead to a common defence.
2. The Union requests the Western European Union (WEU), which is an integral part of the development of the Union, to elaborate and implement decisions and actions of the Union which have defence implications. The Council shall, in agreement with the institutions of the WEU, adopt the necessary practical arrangements.

Other paragraphs contain an explicit commitment not to prejudice the obligations of those member states which are members of NATO, or to stand in the way of bilateral co-operation, provided it is in line with the provisions of the Treaty. Paragraph 6 states that the Article may be revised in the light of experience following a report to be drawn up by the Council in 1996 as part of the Intergovernmental Conference of that year. This suggests that progress towards a common defence policy is likely to parallel that towards a CFSP; in that case the ground was broken with the Single European Act which set the scene for more substantial decisions at Maastricht; in the case of defence, Maastricht set the agenda for more positive moves in 1996. In terms of principle the European Union has made vast strides since the beginning of the eighties when the subject was taboo; it seems safe to predict that more progress will be made in 1996 not least because this is one of the few areas in which a consensus among the member states seems possible.

Article J4 was supplemented by a Declaration, signed by those member states who were also WEU members, in which they agreed to: 'strengthen the role of the WEU, in the longer term perspective of a common defence policy within the European Union which might in time lead to a common defence, compatible with that of the Atlantic Alliance.' The second paragraph states:

> WEU will be developed as the defence component of the European Union and as a means to strengthen the European pillar of the Atlantic Alliance. To this end it will formulate common European defence policy and carry forward its concrete implementation through the further development of its own operational role.

Other provisions set out arrangements for improving co-operation between the WEU and the institutions of the European Union, including synchronization of meetings, a common presidency and links with the Commission in the context of its involvement with CFSP. The WEU Council and Secretariat have been moved to Brussels in recognition of this closer relationship. At the same time co-operation with NATO, whose primacy in defence matters is explicitly recognized, is to be deepened, and WEU members agree to intensify their co-ordination on Atlantic issues with a view to introducing common positions into the process of consultation within the Alliance. WEU's operational role is acknowledged with references to the decision to set up a planning cell, hold regular meetings of Chiefs of Defence Staff and assigning military units to the organization.

In a Declaration the WEU members seek to solve the problem

of overlapping membership by inviting members of the EU to join WEU provided they accept the terms of the Brussels Treaty, or alternatively, to become observers with access to WEU meetings. European members of NATO who were not EU members were invited to become associate members of WEU, with the possibility of participating fully in its activities. As a result of these agreements Greece subsequently joined WEU, Denmark and Ireland became observers and Turkey has become an associate member.

The defence aspects are among the most satisfactory parts of the Maastricht agreements. WEU is recognized as an essential element of the Union and its special function as a link between the EU and the Atlantic Alliance is acknowledged. The agreement is flexible enough to be developed into the fully fledged Common Defence Policy which is accepted as the long-term goal; precedent suggests that like the foreign ministers meeting in political cooperation, the WEU Council will gradually be merged into the Council of Ministers and the distinctions between full members and observers become increasingly blurred. If it did not come up to the hopes and ambitions of President Delors, Maastricht marks a step in his direction for the long term. It was possible because events in Europe had moved on from the Cold War to such an extent that all the parties could see that changes in defence arrangements were necessary. Europe's defence could no longer simply depend on the American dominated Atlantic Alliance, and the development of WEU offered a way forward which had something to offer all the different interests.[5]

The so-called double-hatting provisions agreed at Maastricht were fleshed out by a WEU Council meeting at Petersberg in Germany on 19 June 1992. The ministers declared that they were prepared to assign units from the whole spectrum of their conventional armed forces to WEU for purposes of common defence as defined in the NATO Treaty, and in addition for humanitarian and rescue tasks, peacekeeping and the assignment of combat forces for crisis management including peacemaking. Members would designate those of their forces which could be made available to WEU; these could include forces with NATO missions, provided the SHAPE commanders agreed, and the partners undertook to develop and exercise their forces to enable WEU military units to be deployed when needed. The planning cell would be established in Brussels alongside the Secretariat and become responsible for preparing contingency plans, making recommendations on command and control procedures and maintaining a list of units which might be allocated for specific operations. Steps would be taken to bring Euro-Group and IEPG, both of which had played a role in procurement policy, within the WEU structure.

The relationship with non-WEU members was set out in Part III of the Petersberg Declaration. This bound all members of the European Union and Atlantic Alliance to settle disputes by peaceful means as provided in the UN Charter and other international treaties, refraining from the threat or use of force. To get over the difficulties inherent in the relationship between Turkey and Greece, it was confirmed that the security and defence commitments entered into by members of the WEU and NATO alliances could not be invoked in the case of a dispute between members of either organization. In other words neither Greece nor Turkey could use mutual guarantees in the treaties in a dispute with each other. Observers who accepted these terms could attend meetings and speak on request, associates could take part by common consent in WEU operations on the same basis as full members and were associated with the Planning Cell and communications system. They were also expected to make a contribution to the budget.

The same afternoon there was a meeting with the Foreign Ministers of Bulgaria, Czechoslovakia, Estonia, Hungary, Latvia, Lithuania, Poland and Romania which produced an agreement to intensify co-operation through an annual meeting of foreign and defence ministers and twice yearly meetings of ambassadors. This somewhat nebulous arrangement, which came to be known as the Forum for Consultation, fell well short of the aspirations of the Central and East Europeans and reflects a serious dilemma which has remained unresolved; namely to what extent the new democracies of Central and Eastern Europe are going to participate in Western defence arrangements. If they are indeed to be integrated progressively into the European Union, they will have to enjoy similar defence guarantees to the other member states; not to do so would undermine the whole concept of solidarity and raise questions over investment and other economic activities. From their point of view these countries, with recent memories of Soviet occupation and facing the prospect of continuing instability within Russia itself, see membership of the Western defence system as essential to their security. They clearly prefer NATO, which involves the Americans, to WEU. However the Americans have grave doubts about the wisdom of provoking Russia by bringing its former Warsaw Pact Allies into NATO; and the Europeans, who are reducing their defence budgets, have equally strong reservations over extending defence guarantees in a way that would stretch their limited capabilities to breaking point. There is certainly no disposition to extend full membership of the Alliance to these newly liberalized countries.

As a result the new democracies have been offered a series of palliatives such as membership of the North Atlantic Co-operation Council, links with WEU and more recently the Partnership for Peace Programme which was launched by President Clinton in January 1994 and gives them direct representation at NATO Headquarters and the opportunity to take part in joint exercises. This arrangement falls well short of full membership, though there has been a joint exercise in Poland and much rhetoric about a step by step process. The fact remains that common defence is an essential element in political union and it is difficult to see how these eastern countries can be full members of the EU if they are excluded from its defence arrangements. This must be a major factor in deciding how to develop the Maastricht provisions during the 1996 IGC.[6]

Another area of major uncertainty not addressed by the Treaty concerns procurement and the armaments industry. Article 223 of the Treaty of Rome exempts from Community rules anything to do with the production of or trade in arms, munitions and war material, thus permitting member states to exclude this important industrial sector from the common market. As a result each country has concentrated on supplying weapons to its own forces and although the IEPG has done its best, there has been great reluctance to pool resources. Although there have been some big projects such as the Panavia Consortium, composed of British, German, Italian and Spanish military aircraft manufacturers, which built the Tornado and is now developing the European Fighter Aircraft, the industry for the most part has remained fragmented and dependent on the patronage of the national government. As a result European arms manufacturers have failed to reach the critical mass necessary to finance big development projects, have become less competitive and have failed to enter a number of important specialities such as the manufacture of electronic guidance systems for which European armed forces continue to depend on the United States. Ambitions for a separate European defence pillar ring hollow when it is realized that the Europeans rely on America for weapons supply as well as for intelligence and logistical support, and this must have acted as a constraint on those who argued for a greater degree of independence.

As forces are reduced in size and defence budgets are cut, urgent action is needed if an independent arms manufacturing industry is to be retained and this could be achieved in part by the repeal of Article 223 (which is provided for in the Treaty), which would open up the arms industry to the normal processes of competition. Such a move would end the featherbedding of domestic manufacturers and encourage the growth of transnational consortia, specializing in different types of production. Not only would this produce a better service to the military, but it would reduce the need to maintain capacity by exporting surplus stocks to Third World countries. Whatever the solution, rationalization of the industry on a continental scale is urgently necessary and common systems of procurement which do not favour domestic manufacturers need to be put in place if the European partners are to supply their armed forces with equipment adequate to the tasks entrusted to them by WEU. Common procurement is an essential adjunct to a common defence policy.

The careful references to conventional weapons in the Petersberg Declaration cloak the question of what to do with the British and French nuclear forces in the post Cold War era. So far these have been excluded from discussions of common defence policy; the British deterrent is assigned to NATO, while the French *force de frappe* remains independent of all alliances. The WEU has no nuclear doctrine and while NATO retains a deterrent against nuclear attack, it is increasingly unclear what circumstances if any would justify its use. This aspect of Alliance policy remains firmly under American control. Bilateral contacts have been taking place between Britain and France particularly as regards joint air operations; these are outside WEU and it is not known how far they have involved nuclear issues. The question of the residual European nuclear capability and the circumstances under which it might be used will have to be addressed sooner rather than later.

The fact that issues such as these remain to be resolved demonstrates that in spite of the progress at Maastricht, Europe remains a long way from a common defence policy. After its successes in the Gulf, WEU has failed to have any impact on the Bosnian civil war though it has been co-ordinating naval operations in the Adriatic. Yugoslavia has cruelly exposed the central weakness at the heart of European defence, namely that while there is a willingness to co-operate and a good deal of agreement as to goals, there is no consensus as to how these might be achieved or the political will necessary to take decisive action. The Petersberg Declaration is no substitute for a coherent European military doctrine and without such a doctrine it is impossible to be precise about requirements in terms of forces and equipment. Yugoslavia demonstrates that in defence and security policy the EU falls far short of its ambitions. Mechanisms, however sophisticated, cannot substitute for clear political goals and the determination to achieve them. In particular the prospect of enlargement to the East begs a number of questions about the Union's willingness to see defence co-operation as a necessary accompaniment to economic integration. It may be that this will provide the shock necessary to bring about a redefinition of defence goals beyond simple defence of the national territory and the appropriate changes to the organization of both Alliance and Union which would make them attainable.

10 Economic and Monetary Union: The uncertain dynamic

The idea of a European Economic and Monetary Union (EMU), has long fascinated integrationists and given rise to the darkest suspicions among their opponents. The belief that the ability to issue its own currency is the hallmark of the nation-state is deeprooted, and for governments it constitutes a visible symbol of control over the national economy. For both sides of the argument a move to EMU would be a significant step in the direction of a united Europe in which the independence of nation-states would be diminished.

The symbolism of EMU is all the more potent for its having both economic and political aspects. Looked at from the point of multinational business it has everything to commend it. EMU and its logical consequence, a single currency administered by a European central bank, would remove uncertainty from a significant area of decision-making, would promote cross-border investment and free flows of capital and would tend to reduce inflationary pressures bearing down on interest rates. Transaction costs in the long run would be substantially reduced. Considered against the background of a single market for goods, services, people and capital the logic is all the more compelling; as long as the national governments pursue independent monetary policies the temptation will be present to safeguard short-term competitiveness and shore up employment through devaluation, and with it the risk that others will reintroduce protectionist barriers to shield the domestic economy from 'unfair' competition. As long as there are independent currencies, argue the integrationists, the single market is neither certain nor complete and from the point of view of the consumer and the traveller, it would make sense to be able to use the same money all over Europe without the costly and time-consuming business of currency exchange.

On the other hand there are those who argue that monetary policy can be a factor in competitiveness and devaluation a means of alleviating the harsh effects of deflation and tight monetary policies. The Governor of the Bank of England suggested in a speech in Paris,[1] that the alternative to devaluation could be unacceptably high unemployment leading to mass migration or massive transfers of funds into the weaker economic areas. Moreover without appropriate safeguards, the more profligate governments would be in a position to use the assets of the prudent to inflate their economies and embark on spending sprees, secure in the knowledge that their partners would be required to bail them out. For this reason any form of EMU would have to be accompanied by safeguards which in turn would mean an enhanced degree of control from the centre.

It is however the political consequences of EMU which cause the most difficulty. The former Chancellor, Nigel Lawson, who was a notable convert to the cause of currency stability through membership of the Exchange Rate Mechanism (ERM), believes that a single currency and central bank necessarily leads to a single government. His sentiments have been echoed rather more crudely by Norman Tebbit and Norman Lamont who have asserted that the establishment of EMU would mean the end of British sovereignty and independence. It is this feeling that EMU would mark the crossing of some integrationist Rubicon that has made it the focus of nationalist fears and resentment. If monetary policy was taken away from national governments could fiscal policy and taxation be far behind? The present Chancellor, Kenneth Clarke, has argued that there is no automatic link between monetary union and political integration, citing the previous relationship between the UK and Ireland as an example. This is no doubt correct, but the significance of EMU in binding Europe together should not be underestimated; it would move co-operation to a new level of intensity and send the clearest possible signal that the European partners had committed themselves to an integrationist future.

Others would argue that the idea of monetary independence is an ephemeral concept with only a brief history. For most of the nineteenth century and well into the twentieth, the gold standard acted as an anchor for the world monetary system, producing long periods of stability and consistently low inflation; monetary policy involved ensuring that national

reserves were sufficient to maintain convertibility against gold.
It was only in the post-war era when the gold standard was
replaced by the Bretton Woods system, which was based on the
convertibility of the dollar, that monetary management, backed
up by a battery of exchange controls and restraints on private
borrowing became fashionable. Today the fast growing and
hugely successful economies of South Asia have no monetary
independence as their currencies are linked irrevocably to the
US dollar. Thus Hong Kong, which has a remarkable record
of growth in GNP per capita, simply issues notes on the basis
of its dollar reserves and does not set interest rates, neither do
other Asian tigers such as Taiwan and South Korea; an external
anchor which removes monetary management from the day to
day control of politicians, boosts investor confidence and makes
for economic stability, indeed it could be argued that monetary
independence is a curse rather than a blessing.

If the British see the argument over EMU exclusively in
terms of national independence, other countries have quite
different concerns. The French see EMU as the most appropriate way of preserving a measure of independence by giving them a say in determining monetary policy at European
level, an alternative to government by the Bundesbank. For
them EMU represents a means of reducing German dominance and securing a seat at the top table for themselves. In
1983 the Mitterrand Government decided to link the franc to
the mark and this policy, the *franc fort*, has continued in spite
of high unemployment. Under successive governments the
French have set out at considerable cost to themselves to demonstrate that they are credible partners in a single currency
system which has the principal goal of assuring stability and
they see such a development as being in their national interest. While British public opinion sees any kind of EMU as a
threat to their national independence, the French believe that
it is the best way of preserving theirs.

The Germans believe that monetary union is necessary to
achieve their goal of locking Germany irrevocably into the
European Union and eliminating the possibility of a return to
old habits of nationalism and aggression. It is the culmination
of a process of pooling sovereignty that began with the Coal
and Steel Community of 1951. What better guarantee could
there be of Germany's good intentions than her willingness

to hand over management of the mark, which has been the symbol of her post-war recovery and economic dominance? As the debates following Maastricht revealed, German public opinion is profoundly suspicious of EMU, fearing that it would undermine the mark and put German prosperity in pawn to the southern member states. The Bundesbank under Karl-Otto Poehl and now Hans Tietmeyer, with institutional memories of Weimar, has always been concerned that the subordination of monetary stability to political imperatives could result in inflation. They regard the turbulence that followed monetary union between West Germany and its eastern counterpart as an awful warning of what could happen if there was an EMU with two many discordant voices engaged in its management. This kind of thinking lies behind German insistence on a series of flanking measures which are designed to ensure that the partner governments are not in a position to undermine German monetary prudence. For German public opinion tight control of a single currency by an independent central bank is an essential guarantee that they will not be called upon to make unacceptable sacrifices at the behest of others.[2] For the German political class monetary union can only be justified if it is accompanied by progress towards political union, characterized by common policies for security and defence, strengthening supranational institutions such as the European Parliament, deepening integration to a point where the German genie remains firmly corked inside its bottle.

For the smaller northern member states, that is the Benelux and the Scandinavians, the prize that EMU offers is to be part of an extended area of currency stability. Some of them have tied their national currencies to the mark and thus benefited from the credibility provided by German monetary management, in spite of high fiscal deficits. They are prepared to sacrifice independence for stability and so far at least, there has been no perceptible unrest among their domestic populations despite their abiding suspicion and dislike of German domination. The southern states, Italy, Spain, Greece and Portugal see EMU as a means of providing themselves with the benefits of a strong currency, while looking to the north for the kind of structural investment that will enable them to strengthen their industrial and economic base and thus avoiding the deflationary effects of belonging to a currency union dominated by the mark. For them the issue raised by the Macdougall report of 1977 is critical: this pointed out that developed currency unions such as the United States can only be sustained if the richer areas are prepared to make very substantial fiscal transfers to the poorer regions so that they can cope with the debilitating effects of a non-inflationary currency. In the case of the USA, Macdougall reckoned that such transfers accounted for something close to 30 per cent of the federal budget but this figure is disputed by modern commentators who believe that in the case of the European Union less than 1.5 per cent of GNP would be required. The question is whether the wealthier parts of the European Union are prepared to pay for stability and the promise of economic expansion which would come from keeping the poorer areas in a single currency system.

These questions of political economy are flanked by rather more abstruse questions of political accountability and control of monetary policy. In the days of the gold standard central banks were independent of governments and monetary policy was outside the sphere of politicians who were primarily concerned with the management of taxation in a neutral monetary framework. John Maynard Keynes, writing against a background of economic depression in the aftermath of World War I, suggested that governments could use monetary policy to stimulate economic performance and create employment and growth, ideas which were central to President Roosevelt's New Deal following the great depression in the United States, and this became accepted wisdom as Europeans struggled to rebuild their industrial base after 1945. The Keynesian concept that fiscal policy could be used to fine-tune economies so as to produce beneficial results in terms of growth and job creation enjoyed a vogue in the sixties and seventies, but experience showed that such an approach tended to produce bouts of rapid inflation, alternating with stagnation as the monetary brakes were slammed on to correct overheating. By the end of the seventies Keynesians were in retreat before the liberal sound money approach of Hayek and Milton Friedman. The strict monetarist doctrines of the early eighties and their later derivatives gave credence to the theory that monetary policy should be removed from the control of politicians, who would always be prepared to debauch the currency in pursuit of votes. By the end of the eighties even Chancellor Lawson was advocating that the Bank of England should be made independent.[3]

There is thus a continuing argument between those who believe that monetary policy should be depoliticized by making it the province of central bankers shielded from political interference, whose sole responsibility is to maintain the stability of the currency; and those who continue to believe that central banks must be accountable to the elected representatives of the people whose jobs and prospects are likely to be substantially affected by their decisions. Current political fashion favours the Bundesbank model, an autonomous central bank with its own statute and independent of control by government; this is reflected in the constitution of the European Central Bank set out in the Maastricht Treaty, but there are politicians and economists on the political left who believe strongly that this should be changed, so that monetary policy across Europe would reflect the political priorities of the day. Clearly the view one takes of this issue has a bearing on how one regards EMU as a concept, both in terms of whether it could be made to work and of its overall desirability.

British sceptics such as Norman Lamont claim that a European central bank could not be politically accountable unless there were a single economic policy for it to implement: thus a single central bank leads inevitably to a single government. However it seems clear that the more independent the bank, the easier it would be to sustain separate economic policies, though of course the mere existence of a single monetary policy would tend to promote convergence. Attitudes to EMU are thus conditioned as much by political ideology as by perceived national and economic interest, which explains why the debate has been so complicated; some monetarists who would be expected to believe that monetary policy should be autonomous have attacked EMU with passion as an unacceptable infringement of national sovereignty, as it would remove the Keynesian option of devaluation by individual countries acting alone.

As long ago as 1969, the heads of state and government, meeting in the Hague, commissioned the Werner Report, which set out a plan for the attainment of Economic and Monetary Union; this was adopted in March 1971 and EMU was identified as a goal to be achieved by the end of the decade. In 1972 a system of fixed but adjustable exchange rates known as 'the Snake', whereby currencies fluctuated together in a system of fixed parities, was established under French and German leadership, and the European Monetary Co-operation Fund (ECMF) was established the following year to provide short-term loans to members whose currency was suddenly exposed to speculative pressure. The Snake quickly became a casualty of the 1974 oil shocks and the recessionary conditions of the 1970s. However in 1978 the President of the Commission, Roy Jenkins, floated the idea of a European Monetary System (EMS) which was taken up by President Giscard d'Estaing and Chancellor Helmut Schmidt and finally agreed by the December 1978 European Council. Central to the EMS was the Exchange Rate Mechanism (ERM), a system whereby parities were fixed in the form of a grid with each currency being permitted to float up to 2.5 per cent on either side of its central rate. The ecu is the denominator used to express common prices for agricultural products and for drawing up the EC budget; it is the product of a basket of national currencies, weighted to take account of the relative size of the national economies. If the margin was exceeded, action had to be taken to bring the currency within its fluctuation limits or parities had to be realigned by common agreement. The ERM was designed to provide a zone of currency stability in Europe, following a period of volatility so intense that it had threatened the viability of the common market itself. By coordinating monetary management through a monetary committee the risk of competitive devaluation was much reduced.

During the eighties attempts were made to develop the ecu as an independent currency and these met with some limited success in that it was used as a vehicle for floating government loans and other state transactions. The private use of the ecu never got off the ground. The UK Government, encouraged by the City of London's Committee for Invisibles chaired by Sir Michael Butler, canvassed the idea of developing a 'hard' ecu, in effect a common currency, as an alternative to EMU. Although this idea aroused interest in financial circles, politicians on the Continent viewed it with suspicion as a thinly disguised British attempt to undermine monetary union and so it was never taken up.

The Callaghan Government, mindful of Britain's inglorious exit from the Snake after six weeks in 1972, was profoundly suspicious of any attempt to interfere with national currency management and remained aloof from the EMS on the grounds that thanks to North Sea oil economic conditions in Britain were different to those on the Continent. Their statement that Britain would join 'when the time was ripe' was taken up by Mrs Thatcher who came to power in May 1979, and this became a mantra for expressing British reservations throughout the eighties. The decisive moment for the EMS came in 1983 when the Mitterrand Government was confronted with a choice between the reflationary programme on which it had been elected, a dash for growth, reminiscent of Britain in the early seventies, or remaining within the ERM and accepting the deflationary discipline that it required. Faced with the choice of socialism or Europe, the French President, prompted by his Finance Minister Jacques Delors, opted for Europe and decisively turned his back on the mirage of 'socialism in one country.'[4] Although in its early years the ERM went through a series of realignments, following the Nyborg agreements of 1985 its credibility improved and thanks to a number of technical adjustments and better concertation of policy, the system remained stable throughout the second half of the eighties and played its part in making the Single Market possible.

EMS was always intended to be the first step to EMU, fixed but floating exchange rates being the precursor of the final locking together of parities which would establish a currency union. However the will to move forward was lacking and the system, in spite of its success in minimizing fluctuations, remained in the memorable phrase of Sir Alan Walters, 'essentially half baked'. The successful adoption of the Single European Act and the rapid progress on the 1992 Programme moved EMU back to the top of the agenda, not just because it provided a new and inspiring goal towards which the Community could be pointed, but also because of fears that a renewed bout of exchange rate instability could threaten the achievement of free movement of capital by the target date of 1990. At the June 1988 Hanover Summit, the European Council set up a committee of central bank governors and monetary experts, chaired by President Delors to 'study and propose concrete stages leading towards economic and monetary union'. The committee reported in April 1989 producing a blueprint for progress towards EMU which, echoing the Werner Report, it defined as the irrevocable locking of exchange rates followed rapidly by the replacement of national currencies by a single currency.

The Delors Committee identified three stages leading to the achievement of EMU. The first stage, to begin on 1 July 1990, involved the creation of a single financial area free of exchange controls and other obstacles to the movement of funds (already part of the 1992 Programme), improved co-ordination of economic policies by the ECOFIN Council, and close co-operation between central banks through a committee of their governors. All member states would join the EMS. Meanwhile the next intergovernmental conference, which was required to convene five years after the ratification of the SEA, would prepare the necessary Treaty changes to usher in Stage 2. This would involve the establishment of the basic organs and structures of EMU, notably the European System of Central Banks, and even closer co-operation in the formation of economic and monetary policy, though the national authorities would retain their ultimate independence of action. Fluctuation margins within the ERM would be narrowed prior to the irrevocable locking of exchange rates and the establishment of a single central bank which would inaugurate Stage 3, and this in turn would be followed by the establishment of the single currency.

The Delors Report was highly controversial both in its technical aspects, which many felt were too bureaucratic and prescriptive, and politically in that it clearly pointed the way to a substantial advance in the process of integration. Nonetheless, in spite of the opposition of Margaret Thatcher, it was adopted by the European Council at the Madrid Summit in June 1989 and the British were forced to agree that sterling would be brought into the ERM, provided certain conditions were met.[5] On the strength of this the Heads of Government were able to declare that Stage 1 would begin on 1 July 1990. The Community institutions were requested to adopt the legislation necessary to implement the co-ordination of economic policy required for Stage 1 and to carry out 'the preparatory work for the organisation of an intergovernmental conference to lay down the subsequent stages; that conference would meet once the first stage had begun ...' These decisions were endorsed by the following summit at Strasbourg in December 1989 when the Presidency noted that the necessary majority existed to convene an intergovermental conference to agree the terms of an Economic and Monetary Union at the end of 1990.

The United Kingdom finally joined the Exchange Rate Mechanism on 5 October 1990, a decision that was reluctantly endorsed by the Prime Minister, who continued to resist the idea of an IGC. However at a special summit in Rome on 27–28 October 1990 under the Italian Presidency 11 member states confirmed that the second stage of EMU would start on 1 January 1994, provided that certain objective conditions were met.[6] The European Council decided that steps to implement the third stage would begin within three years of the start of Stage 2. The United Kingdom refused to endorse these conclusions.

The Intergovernmental Conference on Economic and Monetary Union was duly convened in December 1990 and work proceeded through the first half of 1991. The issues were well known and public attention was focused on the parallel conference on political union which gave rise to more obvious controversy. At the Luxembourg Summit in June discussion centred round the degree of convergence between the national economies that would be necessary before Stage 3 could be initiated, and how it would be measured. Jacques Delors said at his press conference that agreement still had to be reached on the role of the ECU, the content of Stage 2 and the budgetary constraints to be imposed on member states who were part of the system. This reflected growing German fears that improvident southern countries, such as Greece, would seek to use the German currency reserves to finance their swelling budget deficits.

The text adopted at Maastricht contained few surprises. It had been obvious for some months that the UK would not be able to make a binding commitment to EMU and so Protocol No. 11, which enabled the UK to reserve her position through an opt-out without wrecking the whole process, had been widely canvassed in advance. In fact the decision to allow Britain to participate in the creation of EMU without having a binding obligation to join was an elegant and statesmanlike solution to the problem. Similar terms were later granted to Denmark.

Of particular importance to Stage 2 of the Delors plan are the rules on excessive deficits contained in Article 104. Instead of the general exhortation to maintain confidence in its currency while maintaining a high level of employment and stable prices, the new Article contains precise rules for the monitoring of deficits and corrective action by the Council if a member state steps out of line. The key paragraphs are as follows:

7. Where the existence of an excessive deficit is decided . . . the Council shall make recommendations to the Member State concerned with a view to bringing that situation to an end within a given period. Subject to the provisions of paragraph 8, these recommendations shall not be made public.
8. Where it establishes that there has been no effective action in response to its recommendations within the period laid down, the Council may make its recommendations public.
9. If a Member State persists in failing to put into practice the recommendations of the Council, the Council may decide to give notice to the Member State to take within a specified time-limit, measures for the deficit reduction which is judged necessary by the Council in order to remedy the situation.

   In such a case the Council may request the Member State concerned to report in accordance with a specific timetable in order to examine the adjustment efforts of that Member State.

Paragraph 9 lists the sanctions that may be applied in the event of non-compliance. These include denial of loans from the European Investment Bank, special deposits and even fines.

The coercive nature of Article 104, which breaks new ground in terms of the supervision of national economies, shows how seriously the member states take deficit control, which is essential to achieving EMU. These draconian rules are intended to assure the Germans that the no-bail-out provision will be as watertight as possible.

The conditions for establishing EMU are set out in Article 109 (j) which calls for the Commission to report to the Council on

the achievement of a high degree of sustainable convergence by reference to the following criteria:

— the achievement of a high degree of price stability; this will be apparent from a rate of inflation which is close to that of, at most, the three best performing Member States in terms of price stability.[7]

— the sustainability of the government financial position; this will be apparent from having achieved a government budgetary position without a deficit that is excessive as determined in accordance with Article 104c (6).[8]

— the observance of normal fluctuation margins provided for by the exchange-rate mechanism of the European Monetary System, for at least two years without devaluing against the currency of any other Member State;[9]

— the durability of convergence achieved by the Member State and of its participation in the exchange-rate mechanism of the European Monetary System being reflected in long term interest-rate levels.[10]

The reports must also take account of the development of the ecu, the results of the integration of markets, current account balances of payments, levels of unemployment, the development of unit labour costs and other price indices. These are all factors in determining whether convergence exists, but it is nowhere suggested that they should be quantified. That the decision to move to Stage 3 is political rather than economic in character is inherent in the fact that it is the Council which has to decide, on the basis of these reports, whether a particular state has met the criteria and whether this is true of a majority of member states. The Council will make a recommendation to the heads of state and government who have to decide whether it is appropriate to proceed to Stage 3. The Commission is required to produce a report on convergence by the end of 1996, and if it is agreed that the criteria are satisfied, Stage 3 can begin for those countries who wish to join, in July 1997. Otherwise the decision is put off until 1999 when, according to Protocol 10, EMU comes into operation automatically on the 1st of January. The heads of government must decide by 1 July 1998 which countries meet the criteria and so qualify to join. In theory the decision to establish EMU by 1 January 1999 has been taken; what remains open is the precise timing of the move to Stage 3 and the determination of which countries are eligible to join.[11] Member states which do not qualify at this stage are treated as having a derogation from the obligations of EMU. This is to be reviewed at least every two years and the heads of government may then decide on a case by case basis that the convergence conditions have been met.

Protocol No. 11 recognizes that the UK shall not be obliged or committed to moving to Stage 3 'without a separate decision to do so by its Government and Parliament'. The UK may notify the Council that it intends to move to Stage 3 before it makes its recommendation to the heads of government, the last opportunity to do this being 1 July 1998.

Article 105 establishes the European System of Central Banks (ESCB), whose primary purpose is to manage the single currency in a way that assures price stability. The ESCB is composed of the national central banks, all of which must be independent of government control, and the European Central Bank itself (ECB), which is a new treaty-based institution. The system is modelled on the Bundesbank and similar to the Federal Reserve in the United States, where a number of regional 'Feds' are responsible for executing the policy decided at the centre. The constitutions of the ESCB and ECB are set out at length in the Treaty and its protocols and represent a victory for those countries, led by the Germans, who advocate an autonomous and politically neutral monetary policy. Though there are various provisions for consultation with the Council and other institutions, the ECB is wholly independent in the decisions it takes to achieve its single overriding objective; whether this would hold up in practice remains to be seen. These new bodies have to be established during Stage 2 and must be ready to assume their responsibilities under Stage 3 by 1 January 1999 at the latest.

Doubts were cast on the viability of the process by the virtual collapse of the ERM in 1992/3. After nearly two years of UK membership, characterized by increasing public hostility and a feeling that the maintenance of high interest rates was prolonging recession, massive currency outflows forced sterling out of the system on 13 September 1992, Black or White Wednesday depending on one's point of view. The exchange rate crisis began with the collapse of the Finnish Mark, then the peseta and the lire were forced out opening the trapdoor for the pound. It was clear that the weaker currencies could no longer be held within a system which offered speculators the certainty of massive gains once confidence was breached. In August 1993 similar speculative attacks on the franc finally forced the effective suspension of the ERM and the extension of the fluctuation margins to 15 per cent either side of the central rate. The attempt to provide fixed but flexible exchange rates had collapsed in ignominy and called in question the whole approach of the Delors Report which was predicated on the survival and consolidation of the EMS all the way to Stage 3.

In fact since the collapse of the system, exchange rates have proved remarkably stable and for the most part currencies have remained comfortably within their original fluctuation margins, perhaps because the looseness of the arrangement has removed the obvious targets for speculation. Moreover since the official fluctuation margins have been widened, the exchange rate part of the convergence criteria is much less onerous, so it is easier for some of the more doubtful candidates to conform. It may be that the collapse of the ERM has made EMU easier by demonstrating that there is no such thing as a half-way house: one either has a full monetary union or a system of competing currencies. Perhaps the best conclusion to draw from the experience of the ERM is that attempts by governments to fix exchange rates by artificial means cannot be guaranteed to withstand the speculative pressures generated by free capital markets when there are doubts about the sustainability of chosen policies.

Stage 2 of EMU duly commenced on 1 January 1994, and the European Monetary Institute (EMI) established by Article 109f of the TEU as a transitional body to prepare the technical aspects of the system began work in 1994 in Frankfurt, which is likely to become the seat of the ECB. The vastness of the technical problems of implementing a single currency is beginning to emerge through the work of EMI and that of the Maas Committee which has been established to bring together the views of practitioners in banking and financial markets, but there is also a widespread feeling that these could be resolved if the governments of the 15 had the will to follow through the commitments made at Maastricht and in the subsequent accession treaties. While the British Government, urged on by its Eurosceptic supporters, continues to express doubts that EMU will ever be achieved except in the very distant future, the view on the Continent tends to be that in spite of the difficulties Stage 3 will commence in 1999. Most people now concede that the 1996 review will not set a date for Stage 3, but will review progress and identify the difficulties that still have to be overcome; in that sense it will move the process forward. Those who believe that EMU is now likely to happen can point to the fact that the European Community, now the Union, has in the past invariably delivered its Treaty commitments. There may have been delays and changes in detail, but the Customs Union, the Common Agricultural Policy, the Common Fisheries Policy and the Single Market have all come to fruition despite the doubts at the time. There is no reason why EMU should be any different if the political will to achieve it is there.

The judgment of the German Constitutional Court on the Maastricht Treaty delivered in October 1992 lays down that there must be a positive vote in the Bundestag before Germany can join a monetary union. This has the effect of giving the Germans their own opt-out and neutralizes automatic commitment contained in Protocol 10 as there could clearly be no monetary union without Germany. German public opinion has shown itself to be increasingly hostile to abandoning the mark and there are questions as to whether the Chirac Government in France will feel able to maintain the *franc fort* policy in the face of high unemployment and possible stagnation. As Ian Davidson points out in the report of the Kingsdown Inquiry EMU depends on the Germans being willing and the French able.[12]

The likelihood is that this will be the case because both the French and German governments see EMU as being in their national interests and because enough of the smaller northern countries believe the same. There is no reason why a majority of eight countries willing and able to move to Stage 3 should not be found when the time comes, even if this means stretching the criteria.[13] It is true that the failure of the ERM in 1992 and 1993 has cast doubts on the ability of the member states to maintain a system of fixed parities, but EMU is a very different matter in that it does not offer the same targets for speculators. Indeed the concept of one powerful currency in a single market of over 400 million people is designed to deter

speculation. Whether the wide variations in economic performance and development would allow EMU to be extended to
all existing and candidate EU members is more problematic,
but if that does not happen the integration between the northern countries who are able to take part is likely to be all the
closer. It would however be foolish in the extreme to imagine
that EMU will not happen by 1999 because the Europeans
will not get their act together. Britain has made that mistake
too often in the past.

We should therefore operate on the assumption that by
July 1998 Britain will have to decide whether or not she wishes
to join those of her partners who are committed to establishing EMU. It is a decision that needs to be taken seriously as
its outcome will determine our relations with the Union for
a very long time to come. It must be clear that if we decide
to opt out of one of the central elements that makes up the
Union structure, it must affect our ability to play a full part in
other areas as well. At best our position would be analogous to
that of Norway or Switzerland: a prosperous enclave on the
margins of the Single Market able to enjoy many of the benefits
of open access, but wholly unable to determine the conditions
under which trade is conducted. We would be in a weak position to pursue our goals of open trade, competition and an
end to state subsidy; those partners who do not share our view
would be in a better position to influence events and policy.
It is questionable whether we could expect to play a central
role in the framing of defence and security policy in Europe
if we were detached from its monetary structures, nor would
we be well placed to encourage enlargement to the East if
others were expected to bear the lion's share of the costs.

The economic case for Britain joining an eventual EMU is
finely balanced, but most economists accept that it would tend
to hold down inflation so that interest rates would be lower,
and provide the kind of stability that is sought by investors. It
may be that Britain would do better if we had independent
control of our own money, though history suggests otherwise,
and conceivable that profligate governments on the Continent
could place our own hard won austerity at risk. However it is
noticeable that many economists and commentators who are
hostile to EMU tend to use economic arguments to justify
opposition which is really based on political considerations. It

is not so much a question of whether or not EMU is a good thing, but rather if there is to be an EMU could Britain afford not to be part of it. There are costs attached to either course of action; there is no doubt that joining EMU would involve a theoretical sacrifice of monetary independence, though in these days of the global economy this may be more apparent than real. Not joining must inevitably lead to increased isolation, a diminishing influence and probably a perception on the part of others that Britain as a nation had failed to come to terms with twenty-first century reality, preferring to cherish the nationalist dreams of a bygone era. This must have a deleterious effect on foreign investment, Britain's own international competitiveness and in the end our national self-confidence.

The decision to join or not to join will have consequences that will affect us for generations to come. Joining EMU would indicate that Britain had finally committed herself to the concept of an ever closer union, not to do so would be an acknowledgement that the attempt at subliminating our imperial past through involving ourselves in the new Europe which Harold Macmillan began in 1960 had finally failed. Either way it will be the biggest decision most of us will have to make and probably deserves to be the subject of a national referendum. If this is to be the case at least we need to make sure that voters understand the issues they are confronted with: they need real information, not the kind of sloganizing and emotional claptrap that has so far passed for debate. Either way two things should be clear: first that EMU is not a mirage that will simply disappear in the heat of economic and commercial reality and secondly that there are costs attached to either choice There is no ideal or clear cut solution.

11 After Maastricht: An uncertain future

The signing on 7 February 1992 of the Treaty of European Union which had been agreed at Maastricht was greeted by sighs of relief in chancelleries throughout the European Union. Although the results fell well short of the ambitions of the integrationists, the Community had held together and there had been significant gains in the fields of foreign policy and defence and in justice and home affairs. The elephant trap of a failed intergovernmental conference, with the member states unable to agree, which had loomed large at different stages of the negotiations had been avoided, and the way seemed clear to turn to the next stage of the European Union's development; that is the accession negotiations with four applicant countries, Austria, Finland, Sweden and Norway.

Enlargement depended on agreeing a new financial settlement which would accommodate the promises for extra cohesion expenditure made in the course of the negotiations to the poorer member states as the price of their signing the new Treaty, and it was with this in mind that on 15 February the Commission published its proposals, known as the Delors 2 package, for raising the expenditure ceiling from 1.2 per cent of GNP to 1.37 per cent for the five years 1993–7. During this period the budget would increase from 63.2 billion ecu to 87.5 billion, mostly as a result of a 31.5 per cent increase in the Structural Funds, bringing them up to 29.3 billion ecu. This sum included provision for the new cohesion fund for Spain, Portugal, Ireland and Greece, the so-called poor four. Agricultural spending would rise by only 12 per cent to ecu 39.6bn so these proposals represented a substantial transfer of resources from north to south, and were seen by the Commission as the price to be paid if enlargement was to proceed. The Delors 2 proposals were to be hotly debated through the year.

The Commission itself was widely seen to have been the major loser at Maastricht; although its competences had been extended in the framework of first pillar, this was no more than a consolidation of initiatives that had already been launched, but which had not previously been embodied in treaty texts. On the other hand the second and third pillars, common foreign and security policy and justice and home affairs, were manifestly intergovernmental in their nature, and although Title I of the Treaty spoke of a single institutional structure this had more to do with the overarching role of the European Council than the Commission, whose sole right of initiative had been confined to EC issues. As far as the new pillars were concerned it was simply an extra player at the table, with no vote, only the right to make proposals and be kept informed. This was a long way from the federalist aspirations of President Delors in his 1989 programme speech.[1] Indeed the Commission itself seemed somewhat chastened; the final paragraph of the 1992 Programme Statement read as follows:

> If a success is to be made of Maastricht and the Single Market, the Commission will have to comply fully with the principle of subsidiarity. Indeed, its future existence depends on this. Beginning in 1992 the Commission, working with the other institutions, will have to establish how subsidiarity is to operate and devise experimental internal procedures to ensure that no attempt is made to regulate matters that are best dealt with at national level and to avoid a surfeit of legislation.[2]

The European Parliament had been frustrated in its ambitions for co-decision, that is equal status with the Council in the legislative process, and had been all but excluded from the second and third pillars. However its powers had been extended through the new conciliation procedure and its influence over the Commission increased, notably in its right to be consulted on the nomination of the Commission President and to vote to approve the appointment of an incoming Commission before it assumed office. The Parliament was particularly incensed by the British opt-out from the Social Chapter, which it believed fatally breached the fundamental principle that Community law, once adopted, should be universal in its application. A two-speed Europe in the field of social policy now seemed a certainty and who was to say that it would not spread to other areas.

While Britain was widely criticized for yet again blocking progress, there was considerable respect for John Major's negotiating skills and a feeling that his more emollient approach might bring Britain closer to the European mainstream, now that he had shown that he was more than capable of fighting his corner. The Conservative victory in the April General Election tended to reinforce this impression. Summing up the Maastricht achievement at a presentation at the Commission offices in London on 28 February, Sir John Kerr, the British Permanent Representative and one of the key negotiators at the IGC said:

> I conclude that it is a very important Treaty and a more important Treaty than the Single European Act. It was achieved without enormous opportunity cost. Its significance in terms of institutional structure is quite hard to divine at the moment, but I would say that the Parliament is a certain gainer and the efficiency of the common foreign and security policy and interior justice are bound to be improved because those who feel strongly that the right institutional structure has been achieved will now have to prove that structure works.

Sir John went on to say that in his view the Treaty would be ratified, and that he did not personally believe that possible difficulties in Denmark, Germany, Ireland and France over specific aspects of the agreement would prevent this. Significantly he did not even mention difficulties in Britain.

This then was the mood in the Spring of 1992 as the Community looked forward to the completion of the Single Market Programme and started work on the Delors 2 package which would provide the finance necessary to implement the Maastricht decisions. No one anticipated that on 2 June, shortly after the House of Commons, by a large majority, had given a second reading to the Bill to ratify the Treaty, the Danish electorate would reject the Treaty by a margin of 1.5 per cent in a national referendum and throw the European Union into total disarray. As the British Prime Minister explained to the House of Commons the following afternoon:

> All twelve members of the European Community agreed and subsequently signed the Treaty of Maastricht. The Treaty amends the Treaty of Rome which can be changed only by unanimity. To come into effect the Maastricht Treaty needs to be ratified by all twelve member states.

Those who criticize the European Union for being undemocratic and trampling on the rights and prerogatives of sovereign states might reflect on the fact that the votes of less than 7000 Danes, citizens of one of the smallest countries in the Union, could bring the whole process of integration to a shuddering halt and in theory at least frustrate the will of 320 million Europeans.

For some weeks there had been signs that the pro-referendum campaign in Denmark was not going well. The coalition government had been in power since 1982 and was unpopular and clearly nearing the end of its term. The Danes had always been reluctant Europeans. As a small country they feared domination, particularly by Germany, and had a traditional distrust of being drawn into alliances which might drive a wedge between them and their northern neighbours.[3] A wealthy country with a highly developed social security system, they feared that their living standards might be undermined by EC social policy and that Single Market rules might force them to compromise their environmental standards. These fears were skilfully exploited by an unlikely combination of anti-market politicians, greens and housewives who saw the Treaty as a threat to the Danish way of life. Matters were not helped by a tactless speech in which the German commissioner Martin Bangemann emphasized the federal character of Maastricht and said that people should not delude themselves into thinking it could be reversed.[4] In spite of all these difficulties the general assumption in Brussels had been that 'common sense' would assert itself and the Danes would vote in favour of the Treaty, though perhaps by a small margin. The shock of rejection was all the more intense for having been unexpected.

It is difficult to exaggerate the psychological effect of the Danish 'No' on both supporters and opponents of the European Union. For a generation of integrationists it had been an article of faith that public opinion was on their side, people in the street looked forward to a united Europe and only national governments and bureaucracies, jealous of their prerogatives, stood in the way. In Brussels there were those who remembered how de Gaulle's standing had dipped sharply in the opinion polls when he defied the Community in 1963 and only recently Margaret Thatcher's anti-Europeanism was thought to have brought about her downfall. Equally the sense that integration was an inevitable process had demoralized the Union's nationalist opponents. Despite grumbling at the minutiae of Community legislation and a feeling that the Commission was exerting too much influence over 'the nooks and crannies of our every day life', no one apart from some political eccentrics seriously believed that the enterprise could fail. it seemed to be the product of an inevitable historical process, destined to succeed in the end. The Danish referendum overturned all these assumptions; suddenly it was the integrationists who were on the defensive and the nationalists who felt they had the wind of public support in their sails. The Commission and the Brussels establishment suffered a stunning blow to their self-confidence from which they have never recovered.

Two days after the result of the Danish referendum was known, the foreign ministers met in Oslo in the margins of a NATO Council. They agreed that the Maastricht agreement could not be renegotiated, but the Danes should be given time to consider their options. The Union could only come into being if all 12 member states agreed, but the Danes were not to be bullied or coerced; their government would have to decide whether to put the matter to a second referendum and if so what assurances it could give the electorate to ensure a different result. These decisions were ratified by the Lisbon Summit at the end of the month, by which time Ireland had held its referendum in which the prospect of increased spending by the Structural Funds produced a substantial majority for the Treaty.

Meanwhile President Mitterrand announced that he would submit the Maastricht Treaty to a referendum in France. This was not necessary as the French Constitution permitted the Treaty to be simply approved by the Council of State, but Mitterrand believed that a successful referendum campaign would restore confidence and momentum to the Maastricht agreements and consolidate his own domestic position. This proved a serious miscalculation; far from rallying support for the European Union, the referendum provided an opportunity for a number of disparate opposition groups to capitalize on public discontent with the Government's record and to give voice to a widespread sense of grievance and disdain for Brussels. Rural France was disgruntled at the prospect of cuts in agricultural support as a result of the MacSharry reforms of the CAP which had been announced in May and this, combined with resentment at EC restrictions on hunting wild birds, was enough to provide the opposition forces with a strong basis of support. Tensions became apparent within the opposition parties of the right, the Gaullist RPR split and leading personalities such as Philippe Sequin and Charles Pasqua became leaders of the 'no' campaign giving it political respectability and clout. The Government was wrong-footed, its campaign was short of verve and conviction and failed to arouse any passion among the French as they lounged on their holiday beaches. The result was desperately close: on 20 September the French voted 'Yes' by a little more than 1 per cent in a mirror image of the Danish result. Indeed at one point after the Minister of Information had declared, 'la France a dit oui!' a rush of late results suggested that he had jumped the gun and the 'no' campaign had actually won.

The narrowness of the victory in France, which, with Germany, traditionally had provided the motive force which drove the integration process forward, did the Union almost as much damage as the Danish defeat. Doubts about the result in France had certainly contributed to turbulence in the currency markets which drove first Italy then Spain and finally the UK out of the Exchange Rate Mechanism on 17 September, leading many to believe that the goal of Economic and Monetary Union laid down in the Treaty could never be achieved.

Events in Denmark and France had an impact on public opinion in Germany where there were increasing fears that EMU would undermine the stability of the mark if it proceeded. The Germans were already beginning to feel the adverse effects of unification with unemployment and inflation figures which by their standards were uncomfortably high. Manfred Brunner, a former official in Commissioner Bangemann's cabinet, launched an anti-Maastricht movement and challenged the validity of the Bundestag's vote to ratify the Treaty in the Constitutional Court at Karlsruhe. The Court did not deliver its judgment until October 1993; it ruled that Germany could not join a monetary union unless there was an affirmative vote in the Bundestag on the specific issue; the decision to join could not follow automatically from the ratification of the Treaty. The judgment strengthened the rights of the governments of the *Lander* to be consulted over further transfers of power to the EU. This will clearly be a factor for the next IGC. The delay caused by the court hearing meant that ironically Germany was the last country to ratify the Treaty which finally came into force in November 1993.

The post-Maastricht backlash was greatest in the UK where a traditionally sceptical public opinion had been whipped up by a long-lasting campaign in certain sections of the press to ridicule the Community and stoke up fears that it threatened Britain's sovereign independence.[5] Memories of Mrs Thatcher's fall were still green and a number of Conservatives in Parliament and the constituency associations saw hostility to Maastricht as the ideal way to demonstrate their loyalty to her and embarrass her successor. A Commons Early Day Motion, calling for the negotiations to be reopened, was tabled in May and attracted over seventy signatures, many of them from newly elected MPs; nonetheless the second reading secured a satisfactory majority and the revolt seemed to have run out of steam. The Danish 'No' galvanized the opponents of the ratification Bill and with turmoil raging on their own back benches the Government decided not to proceed with the committee stage until the situation regarding Denmark was clarified, giving the anti-Maastricht forces and their supporters in the media plenty of time to organize resistance.

The opening of the British Presidency on 1 July found the Community in considerable disarray. By the time John Major convened a special summit at Birmingham on 16 October, it resembled a punch-drunk boxer teetering round the ring after a succession of body blows: the Danish 'No', the postponement of ratification in Britain, sterling's exit from the ERM and the disastrous French referendum campaign. 1992, which should have been a year of achievement and celebration, was turning into a nightmare.

The European Council discussed the Danish proposals for clarification of a number of issues raised by the Treaty, which were subsequently published in the form of a white paper, 'Denmark in Europe'. A declaration was adopted in an effort to reassure public opinion which pointed out among other things that: 'Citizenship of the Union brings our citizens additional rights and protection without in any way taking the place of their national citizenship.'

Other paragraphs called for more openness in the decision-making process, an enhanced role for national parliaments, practical guidelines for applying subsidiarity on the basis that: 'Community legislation must be enforced effectively, and without interfering unnecessarily in the lives of our citizens.'

In a letter to MPs announcing that the Maastricht Bill would now be brought back to the House of Commons, the Foreign Secretary Douglas Hurd wrote:

> No one who listened to the discussion at the Summit about the future of the Community would believe that there is going to be a United States of Europe in our lifetime. Some may regret this, others welcome it, but the idea of a single centralised executive and a single centralised parliament in Europe has perished.

The Maastricht Bill returned to the Commons on 4 November with a motion to proceed to the committee stage. The Government announced that the vote would be treated as one of confidence, which provided the Labour and Liberal opposition parties with the excuse to they needed to vote against. In the event the Government survived with a majority of three, but at the cost of a last-minute concession to one potential rebel that the third reading would not be taken until after the Danes had voted in a second referendum. The rebels had scored a considerable success, demonstrating that they would be prepared to defeat the Government in order to prevent ratification and proceeded to dig in for a protracted and destructive committee stage.

The European Council at Edinburgh on 11–12 December proved a triumph for the British Presidency. The Danish problem was resolved by a declaration which recognized Denmark's right not to participate in Stage 3 of EMU and not to become a member of WEU and thus not participate in decisions and actions of the Union which have defence implications. The section in the Treaty on citizenship was clarified: community citizenship in no sense replaced national citizenship and was determined solely by the national law of the member state concerned. Although the White Paper had raised some doubts, Denmark did agree to participate fully in the Justice and Home Affairs pillar. This package was finally put to the Danish electorate on 27 May 1993 and supported rather grudgingly by 57 per cent of the voters; the immediate crisis was thus resolved though both Britain and Germany had still to ratify the Treaty.

The Edinburgh Council adopted the declaration on subsidiarity which had been promised at Birmingham and this was accompanied by a Commission statement in which it undertook to repeal or withdraw proposals for legislation which seemed to go beyond the new guidelines, and promised to review other measures. A Declaration was adopted on the openness of Council proceedings providing for these to be held in public if the Presidency made a suitable proposal acceptable to the national delegations. The vexed question of the locations of various Community bodies was finally settled and the number of seats in the next European Parliament fixed. There was a Declaration on migration policy and the Commission asked to come forward with proposals on promoting economic recovery.

Most important of all, the member states were able, after much argument, to settle the issue of future financing, considerably reducing the amounts proposed in the Delors 2 package. The Edinburgh agreement covering the period 1993–9, reduced the ceiling on own resources to 1.27 per cent GNP for 1999 whereas Delors had asked for 1.37 per cent by 1997. Structural Funds were cut back to 26.5 billion ecu in 1997 from the proposed 29.3 billion; by 1999 the amount would increase to 30 billion ecu, 35.6 per cent of the budget, a rather higher proportion than originally proposed. Cuts were made in the provision for both on internal and external categories to compensate for these increases. This hard-won agreement provides a basis for financing the Europe Union till the end of the decade though whether it is sufficiently generous to enable it to realize all its ambitions, particularly in the field of enlargement, remains open to question. John Major's ability to squeeze out an agreement on these very sensitive issues at such a difficult time is a tribute to his abilities as a negotiator, skills which were later to be deployed over Northern Ireland and which have seldom been accorded the recognition they deserve.

There was no sense of 'glad confident morning' on 1 January 1993, the day that was intended to mark the triumphant conclusion of the single market programme – rather a feeling of wary resignation. The worst of the crisis was over and the

Union had succeeded in holding together, but its ambitions had been scaled down and the heady optimism and vaulting ambitions of the middle eighties now seemed a distant dream. Baroness Thatcher contemplating the scene from her eyrie in the House of Lords could have permitted herself a quiet smile: Europe did seem likely to be a matter of co-operation between independent sovereign states after all.

In the House of Commons, the Conservative Eurosceptics waged a war of attrition during the committee stage of the Maastricht Bill and the atmosphere became increasingly bitter in the process. Unlike the Conservative opponents of the European Communities Bill in 1971, they were prepared to support the Opposition and defeat the Government on procedural motions, for a time producing a situation akin to deadlock. Discipline went out of the window as the divisions in the Party became increasingly apparent and the Government bobbed and weaved in an attempt to keep its majority intact. It succeeded in so far as there was only one defeat on the substance of the Bill and the third reading was duly carried at the end of May following the second Danish referendum. Following consideration by the House of Lords, which produced a lively debate in which Margaret Thatcher, Geoffrey Howe, Nigel Lawson, Roy Jenkins and Norman Tebbit all featured, the Bill returned to the Commons on 22 July. With the help of Conservative rebels, the Opposition were able to defeat the Government, carrying an amendment which would have made ratification conditional on Britain's signing the Social Protocol. The Government put down a motion reversing this decision the following day, making it clear that this was a matter of confidence and if defeated it would resign immediately, precipitating a general election. This finally brought the rebels to heel and the Government had comfortable majorities of 38 and 40; the Bill completed its Parliamentary stages fifteen months after it received its second reading, at a terrible cost in terms of the cohesion of the Conservative Party and the morale of the Major Government.

The anti-Maastricht backlash which was triggered by the Danish vote on 2 June 1992 nearly brought the European Union to its knees. The intensity of feeling varied from country to country, but throughout the Community there was a feeling that the Danes had blown the whistle on a process of centralization that people felt had gone too fast and too far. Some of this feeling was due to the success of the 1992 Programme which had brought the Community directly into public consciousness for the first time. Regulations designed to make the Single Market effective did impinge directly on cherished national traditions, and increased competition, which it was designed to promote, did cause unease to many small businesses hitherto sheltered by non-tariff barriers to trade. At a time when most governments had been in power for long periods, there was a sense of disenchantment with political process and in a complex technological world conventional democratic practices appeared irrelevant and futile. There is no doubt that many national Parliamentarians felt helpless in the face of a flood of legislation coming out of Brussels which they were expected to rubber stamp so as to implement agreements reached with neither their knowledge nor their consent, and this burgeoning hostility to the EC was picked up by local supporters. This development had been predicted by Jacques Delors in his speech to the European Parliament in the summer of 1988, when he suggested that national parliaments would one day wake up with a shock when they realized how much of their powers had transferred to the Community.

These fears and suspicions of the Community at both parliamentary and grassroots level were massively compounded by the way in which the institutions, went about their business. The Council was guilty of excessive secrecy and duplicity in the way ministers attributed to 'Brussels' the odium for decisions to which they themselves had been party. The constant use of language which portrayed them as the sole defenders of the national interest against an encroaching, unaccountable and alien bureaucracy concealed the fact that for the most part the bureaucracy was composed of their own national civil servants.

The Commission, steeped in the French tradition of *haute adminstration* showed an imperial disdain for public opinion preferring to wring its hands over the misdemeanours of the Council without troubling to put its own case forward in a clear and convincing way. Examples of petty corruption and waste proliferated and the Court of Auditors' repeated criticisms of the financial administration were loftily dismissed. Secure in their permanent status and their tax-free privileges, the Commission services became increasingly detached from opinion outside the walls of their Brussels enclave.

The European Parliament proved far more concerned with advancing its own institutional interests than representing the fears and concerns of the citizens who elected it. To its eternal shame at a time when people throughout the Community were filled with doubts about Maastricht and its consequences for themselves and their families, the European Parliament never had a serious debate at which these fears and criticisms were voiced. With very few exceptions its members failed abysmally to respond to legitimate public concern, leaving it to national politicians to take up the cudgels on behalf of the people who elected them to be their European representatives.

The way in which the negotiations were conducted and the language in which their results were expressed were so impenetrable that no one outside the immediate circle of negotiators understood what Maastricht really meant. Those voters who were called on to express a judgement in the national referenda, had little idea of the issues at stake or how they would personally be affected. The wildest rumours about the content of the Treaty acquired credibility because no one was able to explain what it was about except in terms that were so trivial and meaningless that it hardly seemed worth all the fuss in the first place. Indeed it seems unlikely that the heads of government and their ministers themselves really understood the detail of the Treaty or the nature of the commitments they were undertaking. It was a 'conspiracy of clerks', well-intentioned and even wise, but the essential popular consent was simply taken for granted.[6]

This proved fertile ground for the opponents of the Treaty who were able to play on people's fears and make all kinds of unsubstantiated allegations which could not be easily refuted. It provided an opportunity for politicians opposed to the government of the day to use Maastricht as a stick to beat their opponents so that voters in Denmark and France were almost certainly more interested in using their vote to embarrass an unpopular administration than to express a considered view on the Maastricht Treaty. Even in Britain public attention was focused more on the divisions which the House of Commons debates revealed in the governing party than their political content.

A new Commission took office in January 1994 with a two-year mandate, to make it possible to comply with a treaty provision giving the Commission a five-year mandate coterminous with that of the European Parliament. In future the nomination and installation of a new Commission would follow on from European Parliamentary elections, so that the political composition of the new Parliament could be reflected in that of the Commission; it would also be consulted on the nomination of the incoming president. This procedure was applied for the first time in the case of the Santer Commission which took office in January 1995.

Jacques Delors had been appointed for a further two-year term in June 1992 giving him a total of ten years in office, longer than any previous Commission President. The most important task facing the Community was to conduct the negotiations with four countries, Austria, Finland, Sweden and Norway whose applications had been shelved pending ratification of the Maastricht Treaty and agreement on future financing. Indeed the main argument over future financing had concerned the extra structural spending to be allocated to the four poorest countries to compensate them for additional competition within an expanding Community. Spain in particular had held out for substantial increases and threatened to block negotiations until their demands were met. The Edinburgh Summit settled the issue by increasing the structural funds as a proportion of the budget as a whole and putting extra money into the cohesion fund. As a result it was agreed that the enlargement negotiations could start early in 1993, though they could not be concluded until the Treaty of Union was in force.

The question of enlargement had been contentious for a number of years and had divided those member states who wanted to 'deepen' the Community through additional competences and strengthening the supranational institutions before 'widening' it to take in more member states, and those like Britain and Denmark who saw expansion as a means of diluting the centralizing tendencies of Brussels. Jacques Delors was among those who believed in consolidation before enlargement and as a defensive measure had floated the idea of a European Economic Area in 1988. This involved extending the Single Market to cover the EFTA countries, Austria,

Sweden, Finland, Norway, Iceland, Switzerland and Liechten-
stein without their becoming part of the Community proper
or participating in the Common Agricultural Policy. The collapse of the Soviet Union altered the circumstances: Austria,
Sweden and Finland were all neutral countries bordering on
the USSR or its satellites, so for these three countries accession
to the EC had not been on the agenda. With the Cold War
ended and the Warsaw Pact wound up, neutrality lost much
of its meaning, the main barrier to EC membership was gone
and the attractions of the half-way house of EEA very much
diminished.

The EEA negotiations proved protracted and difficult, the
main issue being how the EFTA partners could be accom-
modated within a single market where the principal decisions
and implementing regulations were made unilaterally by the
EC. An elaborate institutional structure was devised involving
a separate secretariat, a joint competition authority and an
EEA Court, which would adjudicate on disputes between EFTA
and EC partners. The European Court of Justice declared that
this was unconstitutional and negotiations were prolonged by
a year in order to find a satisfactory solution to the problem
of overlapping jurisdiction. Then on 6 December 1992, the
Swiss voted in a referendum not to join the EEA; this led to
the suspension of their application for full membership of the
EC and a reworking of the draft EEA agreements. The EEA
finally came into being at the beginning of 1994 and seems
destined to be a repository for those countries who for political reasons find it impossible to join the Union, but need a
close trading relationship. There are those who believe that
this could be an acceptable alternative for Britain if she were
to leave the Community.[7]

After a slow start accession negotiations with the four applicant countries, Austria, Finland, Sweden and Norway were
finally concluded in March 1994. Much of the groundwork
had been carried out during the EEA negotiations, but difficulties had to be resolved over the adaptation of the highly
protective agricultural regimes of the applicant countries to
the rules of the CAP, agreeing higher standards for environmental legislation than had prevailed in the EC, transit across
the Alps in the case of Austria and fisheries policy in the case
of Norway. In addition there were continuing disputes over

the new members' budget contributions and the additional spending required by the 'poor four' as the price of their agreement to enlargement. After some hesitation the European Parliament assented to the Accession Treaties in its last session before the June 1994 election; referenda in Austria, Finland and Sweden produced narrow majorities for accession but in November the Norwegians voted 'no', repeating almost exactly the result of their previous referendum in 1972. The three new member states joined the Union on 1 January 1995.

The early nineties had been years of recession not least because the Germans were struggling to adapt their economy to the shock of unification and finance the conversion of a rigid command economy to the standards of the free market. As growth slackened unemployment mounted, adding to the general sense of malaise affecting the Community. In December 1993 following a mandate from the Edinburgh Summit, the Commission presented a White Paper called *Growth, Competitiveness and Employment, the Challenges and Ways Forward into the 21st Century*, which set a goal of creating 15 million jobs by the end of the century. This advocated wage restraint combined with a concerted attack on poverty and social exclusion. It set out a programme of action on jobs of which the principal features were greater flexibility, better training and a thorough overhaul of traditional employment policy, designed to prevent long term unemployment. The White Paper called for massive investment in trans-European networks, in information and electronic communications, transport, energy and large scale environmental projects. This would have the effect of binding the Union together and harnessing technological advances to underpin Europe's faltering competitiveness. The capital investment required was 574 billion ecu, of which 20 billion would be provided by the EC using the structural funds and raising new money through Union growth bonds and convertible bonds to be guaranteed by a European investment fund. Predictably the ECOFIN Council regarded the financial engineering part of the proposal as beyond the Commission's competence, but the White Paper was generally welcomed as pointing the way to restoring competitiveness.

The White Paper is interesting in that it demonstrates how far the Commission's thinking moved during the eighties. The emphasis on flexibility in labour markets, focusing on the needs of the unemployed rather than protecting the privileges of those already in work, open markets as opposed to protection and promoting the use of private capital rather than state funded investment, is compelling evidence of Europe's ability to react intellectually to new realities. It remains to be seen whether the Commission's political credit can be restored to a point where it can take the lead in implementing these programmes as it did with the Single Market in 1985, or whether it is to remain hamstrung by suspicion of its centralizing ambitions and the unwillingness of the member states to increase its financial capabilities.

December 1993 also saw the final conclusion of the GATT Uruguay Round after seven years of negotiations and a virtual breakdown in 1991. The Commission was able to rally the member states behind a package which required considerable sacrifices in agricultural support, and the protection of traditional industries such as textiles, in return for increased opportunities for trade in services and intellectual property. By negotiating as a unit the European Union was able to persuade the Americans and other partners to accept an agreement which has the potential to increase world trade, underpinned by a new supervisory World Trade Organization with the authority to police international agreements.

Relations with the countries of central and eastern Europe, now acknowledged as potential members of the Union, pose a moral and economic challenge of vast proportions. The Essen Summit in December 1994 confirmed that,

> The associated states of Central and Eastern Europe can become members of the European Union if they so desire and as soon as they are able to fulfil the necessary conditions,

and indicated that the Europe Agreements were to be the principal means of helping them make the necessary adjustments; an annexe to the conclusions sets out a strategy for developing the economies of the eastern countries in some detail. The European Council also acknowledged that,

> The institutional conditions for ensuring the proper functioning of the Union must be created at the 1996 Intergovernmental Conference which for that reason must take place before accession negotiations begin.

The major question to be resolved by the next intergovernmental conference, which must convene before the end of 1996, is what institutional structure would be appropriate for a European Union of at least twenty member states. Is the answer a loose knit 'multi-track, multi-speed Europe', as advocated by John Major, [8] or does it mean more powers for the supranational institutions to enable them to manage a market of over 500 million people?

Before the accession negotiations can start three basic questions will have to be resolved:

First, will the EC be in a position to proceed to an economic and monetary union and what will be the nature of the deal between France and Germany to make that possible? How far will the Germans be prepared to sacrifice their prized monetary independence in the interests of stability and the trade and political opportunities offered by enlargement?
Second, what changes to the trading structures of the EC itself will need to be made to accommodate the new members and in particular what adjustments to the Common Agricultural Policy are necessary in order to ensure its survival.
Third, what concessions will be made to Spain and other poorer member states who will face increased competition for investment and trade and are currently the principal beneficiaries of the structural funds? How will structural spending be redirected and who will provide the finance?

These vital questions will provide the background to the next IGC and a consensus among the 15 is essential if the European Union is to make progress and carry through the next enlargement.

As the European Union approaches the millennium its most remarkable feature is its ability to survive and adapt itself to changing circumstances. There will always be tensions between member states anxious to protect their national prerogatives and the supranational institutions who for honourable reasons are anxious to extend their power and influence. There is no final balance to be struck; different times call for different prescriptions. The Single Market programme, the great achievement of the eighties, demonstrates the advantages of centralism, the experience of Maastricht and its aftermath shows how dangerous this can be if the institutions lose touch with the people they seek to serve. The next enlargement which is so crucial to long-term stability in Europe will require a massive collective effort if it is to succeed.

The federal idea of a United States of Europe is dead and buried, but few Europeans outside the United Kingdom contemplate a return to a Europe of nation states, pursuing the national interest while attempting to maintain some shaky balance of power. As the pace of change accelerates frontiers look increasingly old fashioned, the process of integration has been driven forward by the needs of industry and commerce as much as by politicians, and there is no reason to suppose that they will wish to return to a system of discrete national markets.

For better or worse the European Union has become a permanent feature of the political landscape; it is for each generation to decide how best to use the opportunities it offers for peace, prosperity and stability in the interests of the different nation states. Whatever the misconceptions of the Founding Fathers may have been, their basic insight, that the pursuit of unbridled nationalism leads to destruction and death and therefore a collective system is essential if European civilization and values are to endure, remains valid. Ever Closer Union implies a constant coming together, but there is no necessary end to the process, merely a constant balancing and rebalancing of our need to live together with a respect for the national traditions and culture which made us what we are in the first place.

Notes

1 'EVER CLOSER UNION'

1. British politicians, unaccustomed to written constitutions, have always had trouble understanding that the Treaties mean exactly what they say. At a conference in Brussels in 1989 Leo Tindemans, the President of the European People's Party Group, was confronted by an angry group of British MPs who declared that Britain had never signed up to Monetary Union. They had to admit that none of them had read the Single European Act the preamble to which identified Monetary Union as a Community goal.
2. See Chapter 9: Defence and Security.
3. The observer, Russell Bretherton, subsequently explained his withdrawal by saying that the Foreign Office thought that 'nothing would happen'. quoted in *The Price of Victory*, Michael Charlton 1983, page 178, cited in *Federal Union: The Pioneers* – Richard Mayne and John Pinder, Macmillan 1990, page 143.
4. 'There had never been much real understanding in the United Kingdom of the depth of the drive towards real unity, as distinct from intergovernmental co-operation on the Continent. Except for a handful of people, no-one really accepted or believed in the feasibility or in the desirability of the Monnet approach to a united Europe.' – Miriam Camps, *Britain and the European Community 1955–1963*, OUP 1964, page 47, cited Pinder and Mayne.
5. Speech at University of Kiel 19 February 1965, cited in *Collision in Brussels* by John Newhouse, Faber & Faber, 1967.
6. Regulation 17/65.
7. The Market Committee of the Danish Folketing has the right to discuss the Government's position before decisions are taken in the Council, if the Minister concerned departs from the agreed stance he has to refer back to the Committee before a decision is reached. This is a cumbersome system but it does provide an effective link between the national Parliament and the EC legislative process.
8. Treaty of Rome, Article 164.
9. 'Mindful of the contribution which the creation of single Community institutions represents for such unification.'

2 THE EUROPEAN COMMISSION

1. *Sunday Telegraph*, 6 November 1994.
2. For a detailed contemporary account of this pivotal moment in the development of the European Community, see *Collision in Brussels – The Common Market Crisis of 30th June 1965* by John Newhouse. Faber & Faber, 1967.

3. Cassis de Dijon, case 120/78.
4. Union des Industries de la Communauté Européen.
5. Conservative Party Conference, Blackpool, October 1987.
6. 'I find it extraordinary that the national parliaments, with the exception of those in the Federal Republic of Germany and the United Kingdom, should have failed to realise what is going on. Ten years hence 80 per cent of our economic legislation and perhaps even our fiscal and social legislation as well will be of Community origin.' Speech to the European Parliament, 6 July 1988.

3 THE COUNCIL OF MINISTERS

1. The author well remembers President Gaston Thorn of the Commission complaining loudly at a meeting with Parliamentarians that Ministers seated at a Council meeting pushed the dossiers prepared by the Council officials to one side to make room for the dossier handed them by their national civil servant sitting behind them.
2. For a full description of the legislative procedures involving Council and Parliament see Chapter 5.
3. As befits a subject of such importance, comitology is hardly mentioned in the textbooks. This account draws heavily on a paper prepared for the Socialist Group in the European Parliament in October 1989 by Richard Corbett, which can be found in the EP Library at Queen Anne's Gate, London.
4. One area in which this sleight of hand is particularly prevalent is social legislation. Conservative ministers have frequently assured the House of Commons and the public that there was a great deal of support for their blocking position, but the others were hiding behind Britain's skirts. Repeated requests to name the member states concerned so that their fellow nationals could be leant on in the European Parliament have received the bland response that Council meetings are confidential and therefore it is impossible to reveal the positions of individual members.

4 THE EUROPEAN PARLIAMENT

1. Belgium 24, Denmark 16, Germany 81, France 81, Ireland 15, Italy 81, Luxembourg 6, Netherlands 25, United Kingdom 81. They were increased by 24 members from Greece in 1983 and 24 from Portugal and 60 from Spain in 1987 bringing the total up to 518.
2. The Conservatives were James Scott-Hopkins, the Leader of the Group, a former junior minister, who had given up his Westminster seat in order to stand for the European Constituency of Hereford and Worcester, Sir Brandon Rhys-Williams, Elaine Kellett-Bowman, James Spicer and Tom Normanton, all of whom remained dual mandate MPs. Lord Harmar-Nicholls was a former Minister, Lord O'Hagan and Lord Bethell had both sat in the nominated Parliament as members of the

House of Lords. The Northern Irish members were Ian Paisley, John Hume and John Taylor, all very experienced.

3. Emma Bonino made the first intervention from the floor, a point of order, in the first directly elected Parliament. In 1995 she became European Commissioner for fisheries policy and promptly took on the Canadians over fishing rights.

4. At the time the European Regional Development Fund, ERDF, the European Social Fund, ESF, and the Guidance Section of the Agricultural Guidance and Guarantee Fund, EAGGF.

5. Isoglucose Case No. 138/79.

6. The kangaroo is best known for its ability to leap over obstacles.

7. The influence of the ad hoc committee, which was chaired by a French trade unionist, Jacques Moreau, on Delors' thinking should not be underestimated. The author was present at a meeting with Fred Catherwood and Delors' deputy *chef de cabinet* in September 1984 at which it was clear that the Single Market was well on the way to becoming the 'Big Idea' of the Delors presidency.

8. Rule 47 of the Rules of Procedure covers 'debates on urgent and topical subjects of major importance'.

9. Examples of this would be the Parliament's support for the British action in the Falklands and attacks on the excesses of the regime in Iran. In both cases the MEPs were a good deal more crisp and decisive than the ministers.

5 THE EUROPEAN COURT OF JUSTICE

1. These are actions by the Council or a member state to void decisions of the Commission (High Authority) which are *ultra vires*, or to require the Commission to act in fulfilment of its obligations.

2. Case No. 141/78.

3. Case 6/64.

4. Case No. 26/62.

5. 'Member States shall refrain from introducing between themselves any new customs duties on imports or exports or any charges having equivalent effect, and from increasing those which already apply in their trade with each other.'

6. Case No. 92/78.

7. Case No. 213/89.

8. 1990 2 AC 85.

9. See the Waterkeyn Case, 314–16/81: 'If the Court finds.... that a Member State's legislation is incompatible with obligations which it has under the Treaty the Courts of that State are bound by virtue of Article 171 to draw the necessary inferences from the judgment of the Court . . . the rights accruing to individuals derive not from that judgment but from the actual provisions of Community law having direct effect in the internal legal order.'

10. IBM Case No. 60/81.

11. Case No. 85/76.

12.   *M H Marshall* v. *Southampton and South West Area Health Authority*, Case No. 152/84.
13.   Case No. 76/207.
14.   Case No. 262/88 [1990].

6   THE ROAD TO MAASTRICHT

1.   The opening paragraph of the Presidency's conclusions on Monetary Union reads as follows: 'The European Council recalls that, in adopting the Single Act, the Member States confirmed the objective of progressive realisation of economic and monetary union.' *Bulletin of the EC*, June 1988.

2.   This finally saw the light of day in a Treasury paper, 'An Evolutionary Approach to Economic and Monetary Union', published in November 1989. This built on the Lawsonian idea of competing currencies and suggested stopping short after the completion of Stage 1 allowing each currency to find its natural level within a strengthened EMS. By the time it appeared events had already moved on.

3.   'Ever since Britain joined the Community we have seen European Institutions placing a systematically different interpretation on texts than those we accepted. Vague declarations which we assumed at the time had no practical implication, were subsequently cited to justify the extension of Community powers into fresh areas of national life.' Extract from 'The Path to Power', *Sunday Times*, 28 May 1995.

4.   As Charles Moore, then editor of the *Sunday Telegraph*, put it on a BBC *Any Questions* programme, 'Jacques Delors wants to rule our country.'

5.   The author recalls being at a dinner with John Kornblum, then Deputy US Ambassador to NATO, in February 1990 when he explained that the many different US intelligence scenarios for the break-up of the Warsaw Pact had one insight in common. Of all the satellites, East Germany was most firmly embedded in the Soviet system, and the one the Russians themselves would least want to give up. Unification could therefore only come at the very final stages of detente when all other East–West problems had been resolved. The fact that it had occurred at the beginning of the Soviet break-up took everyone completely by surprise.

6.   Lecture at St Antony's College Oxford, 11 November 1992. This may be compared with Margaret Thatcher's concept of 'Willing and active co-operation between independent sovereign states' – Bruges, 1988.

7.   The first paragraph of Article B which covers the role of the first pillar reads as follows: 'to promote economic and social progress which is balanced and sustainable, in particular through the creation of an area without internal frontiers, through the strengthening of economic and social cohesion and through the establishment of economic and monetary union, ultimately including a single currency in accordance with the provisions of the Treaty.'

8.   'Police cooperation for the purposes of preventing and combating terrorism, unlawful drug trafficking and other serious forms of interna-

tional crime, including if necessary certain forms of customs cooperation, in connection with the organisation of a Union-wide system for exchanging information within a European Police Office [EUROPOL].'

7 THE COMPETENCES OF THE UNION

1. The Treaty of European Union (TEU), as the Maastricht treaty is correctly styled, is a separate treaty between the member states which establishes the Union and recognizes the existence of the European Council. Title V of this Treaty covers the Common Foreign and Security Policy and Title VI provisions on co-operation in the fields of justice and home affairs. Titles II, III and IV contain amendments to the existing Treaties covering the EC, ECSC and EURATOM which remain distinct from the TEU itself.
2. Article 100c provides for a common list of third countries whose nationals require visas in order to enter the EU and for a common visa format. This was a significant exception to the generally intergovernmental character of the Maastricht agreements.
3. Article 123.
4. Article 43.
5. Speech at the Guildhall, London, 4 May 1995.

8 THE COMMON FOREIGN AND SECURITY POLICY

1. The separation of EPC from the Community as such was dramatically illustrated at Parliamentary Question Time. When questions to the Foreign Ministers meeting in Political Co-operation was called immediately following questions to the Council of Ministers, the Council Officials who were Community civil servants removed themselves from the benches, leaving the President in Office alone in the House with one or more national officials.
2. Speech to Les Grands Conferences Catholiques, June 1978, published by the European Conservative Group.
3. Gaston Thorn as Foreign Minister of Luxembourg was despatched on a mission to the Middle East during the Luxembourg Presidency and found that there was no one to meet him at Tel Aviv Airport. Luxembourg had no mission in Israel.
4. 19 November 1981, *Bulletin of the EC* 11, 1981 para 1.2.2.
5. This clearly referred in particular to the United Nations Security Council where Britain and France only were permanent members.
6. A high-level Japanese trade delegation were taken to Koratron, widely regarded as the showpiece of East German technological prowess. They were also shown round the Pergamon Museum with its unique collection of Greek antiquities from Asia Minor. Asked about the trip they said they had been shown round two museums, one technological and one antiquarian and both had been very interesting. They apparently were not joking.

7. Poland, Hungary, Bulgaria, Romania, Lithuania and more recently Estonia all now have governments dominated by former Communists.

8.   1. The Council shall decide on the basis of general guidelines from the European Council, that a matter should be the subject of joint action.
       Whenever the Council decides on the principle of joint action, it shall lay down the specific scope, the Union's general and specific objectives in carrying out such action, if necessary its duration and the means, procedures and conditions for its implementation.
   2. The Council shall when adopting the joint action, and at any stage during its development, define those matters on which decisions are to be take by a qualified majority. (Article J.3)

9. Second Report, *Europe after Maastricht*, 29 April 1993, para 35.
10. *Le Monde*, 28 June 1991.
11. *Financial Times*, 1 July 1991.
12. *Financial Times*, 16 January 1992.

9   DEFENCE AND SECURITY

1. 'Any Member State may take such measures as it considers necessary for the protection of the essential interests of its security which are connected with the production of or trade in arms, munitions and war material; such measures shall not adversely affect the conditions of competition in the common market regarding products which are not intended for specifically military purposes.' Treaty of Rome, Article 223 (b).
2. SEA Article 30.6 (a) and (c).
3. Alastair Buchan Memorial Lecture, 7 March 1991.
4. *Financial Times*, 15 April 1991.
5. The defence arrangements which emerged from Maastricht paralleled to a remarkable extent the recommendations of a working group of Conservative MEPs. Their findings, published in a pamphlet, 'Defence and Security in the New Europe', were published at the beginning of 1992 and were the product of more than a year of hearings with a wide range of experts.
6. The ambivalence of the European attitude to the new democracies is well illustrated in the following quotation from Dr Willem van Eekelen, then Secretary General to the WEU:

> Clearly, automatic security guarantees will not be on offer either in WEU or in NATO for some time to come, not even perhaps by the year 2000. In the meantime a substantial and evolving status would be a major step forward, certainly a decisive one towards those countries being allowed to join the European Union. They will be associated with the process of building the political institutions of the Union. Their participation in the Petersberg missions could only

increase their status in the Partnership for Peace. Because they recognise the primacy of politics in those special relationships, the European Union and the Alliance cannot shirk their duty of showing them a minimum of solidarity. (Royal Institute of International Relations, January 1994)

10 ECONOMIC AND MONETARY UNION

1. 29 January 1995.
2. Herein lies an interesting paradox: in Britain it is possible that people could be persuaded to accept monetary union if they could be reassured that it would not lead to a European government, which is the interpretation they place on political union. For the Germans monetary union is unacceptable unless accompanied by a political union through which they would have some oversight of the economic policy-making of their partners in default of adequate guarantees that they would not have to 'bail them out' in the event of a crisis in their reserves.
3. The arrangement whereby the minutes of meetings between the Chancellor and the Governor of the Bank of England are published go some way towards establishing the role of the Bank as an independent partner in setting monetary policy.
4. It is easy to forget at this distance that the Mitterrand strategy was based on a realignment of the left. The 1981 French Government contained four Communist ministers, the first time this had happened since the Second World War.
5. See Chapter 6 for an account of the Madrid Summit.
6. The objective conditions were:

   — completion of the Single Market;
   — ratification of the Treaty on EMU;
   — measures set in motion to ensure the independence of the new central monetary institution and that member states are no longer allowed to finance deficits by increasing the money supply.

7. Protocol No. 6 states that the criterion shall be a rate of inflation that does not exceed the rates of the three best performing member states by more than 1.5 per cent.
8. Protocol No. 5 states that the benchmarks for measuring deficits are that the annual budget deficit should be no more than 3 per cent and overall government debt no more than 60 per cent of GNP.
9. Defined in Protocol No. 6 as operating within the fluctuation margins for two years without severe tensions.
10. Protocol No. 6 establishes that the standard is a long-term interest rate that does not exceed the three best performing member states in terms of inflation by more than 2 per cent over the prior year.
11. See Protocol No. 10 which declares that the Maastricht treaty amounts to an irreversible decision to establish EMU by 1 January 1999 at the latest with the ECB and ESCB ready to start functioning on this date. The non-convergent states cannot prevent the others from going ahead.

12. Report of the Kingsdown Inquiry into the implications of Monetary Union for Britain, published by Action Centre for Europe Ltd, June 1995.
13. The most likely seven are Germany, France, Holland, Belgium, Luxembourg, Ireland and Austria, with Sweden, Finland, Italy, Spain and Portugal some way behind. Greece is unlikely to be ready.

11 AFTER MAASTRICHT

1. See Chapter 6.
2. *Bulletin of the EC*, Supplement 1/92, page 45.
3. The Danish attitude to relations with their neighbours has its roots in the war with Prussia over Schleswig Holstein in 1862. This has produced a national phobia that Denmark is bound to be the loser in any conflict because of her small size. The belief that Schleswig Holstein was lost to German aggression because of the indifference of other European powers to the needs of a small peripheral country survives to this day and explains Danish suspicion of Germany and her distrust of WEU which draws her into a Continental as opposed to an Atlantic alliance.
4. John Major for one believed that the Bangemann speech actually tipped the balance in the Danish referendum and in private conversation was wont to blame him personally for all the difficulties that followed. The speech certainly ended any hopes Martin Bangemann may still have cherished of becoming President of the Commission.
5. This was not an argument that appealed to the Sovereign herself. In her speech to the European Parliament on 12 May 1993, Queen Elizabeth said: 'Decisions need to be taken as close to the citizen as is compatible with their success. But at the same time we have to strengthen the ability of Europeans to act on a European basis where the nature of the problem requires a European response. That was the necessary balance struck at Maastricht.'
6. The point about heads of government having only the vaguest notion of the content of the negotiations was made privately by Phillipe de Boissieux, a senior Quai d'Orsay official who was a member of the of the inner negotiating team and subsequently France's Permanent Representative. Over lunch at a CEPS conference in 1994 he said that only three or four people, one of whom was himself, really understood what was in the texts. Heads of government were briefed on specific items but not the whole Treaty.
7. For instance Norman Lamont in his speech to the Selsdon Society in Bournemouth, October 1994.
8. Speech at Leiden University, October 1994.

Glossary

CAP	Common Agricultural Policy.
CET	Common External Tariff.
CFP	Common Fisheries Policy.
CFE	Treaty on the reduction of Conventional Forces in Europe.
CFI	Court of First Instance.
CFSP	Common Foreign and Security Policy, the second Maastricht pillar.
COREPER	Committee of Permanent Representatives (*Comité des Représentants Permanents*).
CSCE	Conference on Security and Cooperation in Europe, following the Treaty of Paris renamed OSCE – Organisation replaces Conference.
EAGGF	European Agricultural Guidance and Guarantee Fund, also known as FEOGA after its French acronym.
EBRD	European Bank for Reconstruction and Development.
EC	European Community, following the adoption of the Single European Act, 'economic' was dropped from the title of the EEC.
ECB	European Central Bank.
ECJ	European Court of Justice.
ECOFIN	Council of Economic and Finance Ministers.
ECSC	European Coal and Steel Community established by the Treaty of Paris, 18 April 1951.
ECU	European Currency Unit.
EDC	European Defence Community, rejected by the French National Assembly, August 1954.
EEA	European Economic Area, now composed of Norway, Iceland and Liechtenstein plus the EU.
EEC	European Economic Community established by the Treaty of Rome, 25 March 1957.
EFTA	European Free Trade Area, the original seven were UK, Norway, Denmark, Sweden, Portugal, Switzerland, Ireland.
EIB	European Investment Bank.
EMAC	European Parliament Committee for Economic and Monetary Affairs and Industrial Policy.
EMCF	European Monetary Cooperation Fund.
EMI	European Monetary Institute.
EMS	European Monetary System.
EMU	Economic and Monetary Union.
EPC	European Political Cooperation.
ERDF	European Regional Development Fund.
ERM	Exchange Rate Mechanism.
ESF	European Social Fund.
ETUC	European Trade Union Confederation.

EU	European Union, established by the Maastricht Treaty (TEU) and comprising three pillars: European Community (EC), Common Foreign and Security Policy (CFSP) and Justice and Home Affairs (JHA) under the aegis of the European Council.
EURATOM	European Atomic Energy Community (EAEC) established by the Treaty of Brussels, 17 April 1957.
EUROPOL	European Police Office, based in The Hague.
ICBM	Intercontinental ballistic missile.
IEPG	Independent European Programme Group, responsible for co-ordinating the specification of military equipment, now absorbed into WEU.
IGC	Intergovernmental Conference.
IMPS	Integrated Mediterranean Programmes, special programmes established in 1986 for Southern Italy, Greece, Corsica and the French Overseas Territories to soften the competitive blow of the accession of Spain and Portugal.
INF	Intermediate Nuclear Forces.
JHA	Co-operation in the fields of Justice and Home Affairs, the third Maastricht pillar.
NATO	North Atlantic Treaty Organization, established by the Treaty of Washington, 4 April 1949.
OECD	Organisation for Economic Cooperation and Development, 'development' has now been dropped from the title.
OJ	*Official Journal of the European Community.*
PHARE	Aid to promote the economic liberalization of Poland, Hungary, Romania, and now Bulgaria, Slovakia and Albania.
UN	United Nations Organisation.
UNICE	Federation of European Industry (*Union des Industries de la Communauté Européen*).
SEA	Single European Act, signed at Luxembourg and The Hague, February 1986.
SHAPE	Supreme Headquarters Allied Powers in Europe.
SIGINT	Signals Intelligence, the NATO acronym for electronic military surveillance.
SLCMS	Submarine Launched Cruise Missiles.
START	Strategic Arms Reduction Treaty.
TACIS	Technical Assistance for the Commonwealth of Independent States.
TASMS	Tactical Air to Surface Missiles.
TENS	Trans-European Networks.
TEU	Treaty of European Union signed at Maastricht, 7 February 1992.
VAT	Value Added Tax.
WEU	Western European Union, established originally as the Brussels Treaty of Economic, Social and Cultural Collaboration and Collective Self Defence, 17 March 1948.

Index